Decentralization for Satisfying Basic Needs

An Economic Guide for Policymakers

Second Edition

A volume in
Research on Hispanic and Latino Business

Series Editor:
Esther Elena Lopez-Mulnix and Michael Mulnix
Antioch University-Santa Barnara

Research of Hispanic and Latino Business

Esther Elena Lopez-Mulnix and Michael Mulnix, Series Editors

Decentralization for Satisfying Basic Needs: An Economic Guide for Policymakers, Second Edition (2010)
by J. Michael McGuire

Descentralizacion para Satisfacer Necesidades Basicas: Una Guia Economica para Profesionales (2009)
by J. Michael McGuire

Decentralization for Satisfying Basic Needs: An Economic Guide for Policymakers (2005)
by J. Michael McGuire

Decentralization for Satisfying Basic Needs

An Economic Guide for Policymakers

Second Edition

---

by

J. Michael McGuire
University of the Incarnate Word

IAP

Information Age Publishing, Inc.
Charlotte, North Carolina • www.infoagepub.com

Library of Congress Cataloging-in-Publication Data

McGuire, J. Michael (James Michael), 1940-
Decentralization for satisfying basic needs : an economic guide for policymakers / by J. Michael McGuire. — 2nd ed.
p. cm. — (Research on Hispanic and Latino business)
Includes bibliographical references and index.
ISBN 978-1-60752-410-6 (paperback) — ISBN 978-1-60752-411-3 (hardcover) — ISBN 978-1-60752-412-0 (e-book)
1. Poverty—Latin America. 2. Decentralization in government—Latin America. 3. Economic assistance, American. 4. Latin America—Economic conditions. I. Title.
HC130.P6M34 2010
362.5'56098—dc22

2009053670

Printed in the United States of America

For
Patience
and
Don Serapio

CONTENTS

LIST OF TABLES, FIGURES, AND BOXES

TABLES

FIGURES

BOXES

ABBREVIATIONS

BEA: Bureau of Economic Analysis

CEDEMUN: Centro Nacional de Desarrollo Municipal

CIDE: Centro de Investigación y Ciencias Económicas

CIESN: Center for International Earth Science Network, Colombia University

COPLADET: Comité de Planeación del Estado de Tlaxcala

DAC: Development Assistance Committee

FAIS: Fondo de Aportaciones para la Infraestructura Social

FAISE: Fondo de Aportaciones para la Infraestructura Social Estatal

FAISM: Fondo de Aportaciones para la Infraestructura Social Municipal

FGP: Fondo General de Participaciones

FY: Fiscal year

GDP: Gross Domestic Product

GNI: Gross National Income

GNP: Gross National Product

HDI: Human Development Index

IDA: International Development Association

IFAD: International Fund for Agricultural Development

IFC: International Finance Corporation

IFPRI: International Food Policy Research Institute

IMF: International Monetary Fund

IMF WEO: International Monetary Fund World Economic Outlook
INEGI: Instituto Nacional de Información Geográfica y Informática
MCA: Millennium Challenge Account
MCC: Millennium Challenge Corporation
NGO: Nongovernmental Organization
ODA: Official Development Assistance
OECD: Organization of Economic Cooperation and Development
PPP: Purchasing Power Parity
SEGOB: Secretaría de Gobernación de México
SHCP: Secretaría de Hacienda y Crédito Público
UNESCO: United Nations Educational Scientific and Cultural Organization
UNICEF: United Nations International Childrens' Emergency Fund
UNDP: United Nations Development Program
USAID: United States Agency for International Development
YCELP: Yale Center for Environmental Law and Policy

PREFACE

More than one in every five Latin Americans lives on less than $2 a day. Countless more are eking out a living with only slightly more income. In addition, Latin America is the most unequal region in the world. Given the region's low per capita income (less than one fifth that of the United States), severe inequality implies dire poverty for those at the bottom of the income scale.

The best solution to poverty and inequality includes the satisfaction of the basic needs of the poor. Satisfying basic needs such as education, health care and nutrition enhance the productivity of the poor. This imparts an indispensable opportunity to earn an income sufficient to emerge from poverty and to live a full life.

Satisfying basic needs does much more than give the *poor* an opportunity to live a full and productive life. It also develops the *nation*. Improving the productivity of the poor increases the quantity and quality of goods and services available for general consumption. It lowers costs and prices. It increases profits. Satisfying basic needs is an approach to development, not just of the poor, but also of the nation.

Decentralization is a process of transferring taxing and spending decisions from the central government to subnational entities like states and municipalities. Decentralization can contribute greatly to the satisfaction of basic needs of the poor in many ways. For example, one of the most debilitating aspects of poverty is voicelessness. Bringing government closer to the poor through decentralization can give excluded people

Decentralization for Satisfying Basic Needs: An Economic Guide for Policymakers, 2nd Edition
pp. xiii–xv

voice and power over the basic goods and services provided by government. This can enhance the quality of delivery and the sustainability of those goods and services.

However, decentralization is not an automatic cure-all for improving the delivery of basic goods and services provided by government. For example, decentralizing taxing and spending to corrupt local governments can actually reduce the amount of funds available for satisfying basic needs.

Decentralization is a *process* that must take into account both the strengths and weaknesses of each level of government. There are many possible degrees of decentralization, each of which takes advantage of some strengths and compensates for some weaknesses. The challenge to policymakers is to design the *process* of decentralization that is most effective in the imperfect world in which we live.

The challenge addressed in this book is designing the degree of decentralization that is most effective in satisfying the basic needs of the poor, given the country's real-world circumstances. The approach is to present a model of decentralization that identifies the key agents in the process and the ideal relationships between those agents. Next, case studies of decentralization at work in the real world are presented and analyzed in light of the model. The analyses identify strengths and weaknesses of each case, and generate recommendations for taking the next step in the decentralization process.

The aim of this book is to help the reader who wishes to use decentralization to help implement a basic needs approach to development to advance his or her own analytical skills of doing so. The aim is not to "give the answer," but rather to provide insight into decentralization *as a process* and to help practitioners develop skills in designing their own decentralization programs.

The focus is on satisfying basic needs in Latin America, but the analytical approach is applicable to other regions of the world. The book presupposes no background in economics, but courses in the principles of economics, Latin American economics and public finance would enrich understanding. The book should be helpful to public officials and citizens involved in setting public policy for development. It could serve as a supplementary text for students of Latin American economics, development economics, political economy, public administration, political science, Latin American studies, and related fields.

The second edition of the book includes two new chapters that cover the important but often neglected topic of taxation for inclusive development. Chapter 8 analyzes the influential tax advice of the World Bank in terms of its effect on the satisfaction of the basic needs of the poor and generating an inclusive development process. Appendix B of Chapter 8 presents an empirical analysis in support of the chapter's thesis that the World Bank's recommendation of regressive taxation inhibits inclusive development. Chapter 9 analyzes the effects of the World Bank's tax advice on El Salvador's tax reform and development process. Two other chapters have been extensively updated: Chapter 6 records and analyzes the rapid evolution of Mexico's *Oportunidades* program for health, education and nutrition, and Chapter 10 follows the progress of the United States' innovative program for foreign aid, The Millennium Challenge Account. Throughout the book, tables and references have been updated.

I am deeply indebted to many persons whose support has been essential to completing this work. The advice and encouragement of my wife, Dr. Patience Lea McGuire, provided many valuable insights and kept the completion of the manuscript on schedule; she utilized her amazing computer skills to produce the figures of Chapters 3, 4 and 10. My research assistant, Chrystal Alexander, updated the tables of Chapter 1. Juan Daniel Lopez Barroso, generously arranged interviews with public officials in Mexico that otherwise would have been impossible. Juan Daniel Lopez Barroso de Flon, *director general* of the Mexico City newspaper, *Zona Norte*, granted insightful interviews, arranged many interviews with public officials and others, helped to finance four trips to Mexico City and provided indispensable transportation. Patricia Andrade, Reporter, *Zona Norte*, generously shared with me her vast experience of Mexico, arranged interviews with Mexican public officials and persons suffering the consequences of poverty, and enriched the interviews by her presence. A sabbatical from the University of the Incarnate Word made time available for completion of the manuscript. Title V grants from the U.S. Department of Education helped to fund travel to El Salvador and to Mexico, and to purchase materials used in the project. I am indebted to many scholars whose work in development economics served as the foundation upon which this book is built. A Fulbright Fellowship to the Central American University (UCA) of San Salvador, El Salvador, annual invitations from the UCA to return for teaching and research, and the help of many Salvadoran scholars and friends have greatly increased my understanding of Latin America, its poverty and inequality, and the basic needs approach to development. The Jesuit priests of the university have helped inspire me to remain faithful to the cause of improving society through giving the poor more opportunity to live full lives. Any weaknesses of the book are entirely my own responsibility.

INTRODUCTION

Give them bricks and they will build their own houses.

—Anonymous

A small community named *Calle Real* demonstrates the power of satisfying the basic needs of the poor. The residents of *Calle Real* migrated from a rural conflictive zone to the outskirts of San Salvador, the capital city of El Salvador, early in the country's 12 year civil war (1979-1991). They arrived destitute—with nothing but that which they could carry.

Their church gave them land. A foundation in Canada gave them bricks and mortar. With these resources in hand, the refugees built their own houses. The community met on Sunday afternoons to plan the development. The housing lots were distributed by lottery. Construction tasks for the week were distributed among community members. Together, they constructed the houses one by one. They planted flowers in front of their homes. Children play in the streets.

These houses—which are far better than the typical shanties occupied by low-income Salvadorans—have had a profound impact on the people of *Calle Real*. They help to keep parents and children healthy, both mentally and physically. Good health helps parents to work regularly and to earn a better living. Good health helps children to attend school regularly, to learn, and to prepare to earn a decent living in the future.

"Give them bricks, and they will build their own houses." This is a metaphor describing a basic needs approach to development. In *Calle Real*

Decentralization for Satisfying Basic Needs: An Economic Guide for Policymakers, 2nd Edition
pp. xvii–xix

other basic needs were satisfied by generous donors, and the community has flourished. Satisfying basic needs is like giving people bricks. It creates an indispensable opportunity to progress. They will not fail to seize it.

Satisfying basic needs does more than free the poor to improve the quality of their lives. It also boosts the economy of the *nation*. Making the poor more productive by repeating the experience of *Calle Real* speeds the growth of GDP, so that the nation has more goods and services available for consumption. Greater productivity of the poor lowers the costs of production. This, in turn, increases profits and lowers the prices that everybody pays. Satisfying basic needs tends to lower taxes by reducing the need for public welfare expenditures and for public expenditures to combat crime. Satisfying basic needs is not primarily a welfare program, but rather an approach to national development. The best approach to national development includes satisfying the basic needs of the poor.

Governments supply many basic goods and services to the poor such as primary education, health care, potable water, sewerage, sanitation and housing. Decentralization—the process of transferring taxing and spending decisions from the central government to subnational entities like states and municipalities—can be a great help to do it more effectively.

For example, bringing government closer to the people can help to overcome the bane of poverty, voicelessness. Giving more voice to the people, can improve planning and help government tailor services to meet the special needs of their jurisdictions. Greater voice can improve monitoring and the accountability of government to the people. Greater voice can improve the sustainability of development projects.

Despite its potential benefits, decentralization is not an automatic cure-all for effective service delivery. If, for example, a pro-poor central government decentralizes taxing and spending to local governments that are captured by elites, the voice of the poor may never be heard, and the supply of basic goods and services to the poor may actually diminish. Decentralization is a multi-stage process that must be tailored at each stage to take advantage of society's strengths, to compensate for its weaknesses, and to prepare to take the next step forward.

The purpose of this book is to help practitioners, both governmental and nongovernmental, to develop skills in designing and using decentralization to satisfy the basic needs of the poor more effectively. The aim is not to "give the answer," but rather to provide insight into decentralization *as a process* and to help practitioners develop skills in designing their own decentralization programs. The ultimate objective is equitable and sustainable development for all.

Chapter 1 shows the need to satisfy basic needs by describing the poverty and inequality that afflict Latin America. Chapter 2 presents the basic needs approach to development as an essential means of addressing that poverty and inequality. Chapter 3 presents a model of service delivery by the government. The model identifies key agents of the service delivery process, and it describes the relationships between the agents that make that service delivery effective. Chapter 4 extends the model of service delivery to develop a model of decentralization.

Chapters 5-10 present six case studies of decentralization at work. Each chapter describes a distinctive style of decentralization that was developed in response to real world circumstances. The chapter then uses the decentralization model to identify the case's strengths and weaknesses, and to recommend the next step forward in the decentralization process. The hope is that practicing theoretical analysis of real world cases will develop the readers' skills of designing and implementing a decentralization process that effectively promotes a basic needs approach to development.

PART I

INCLUSIVE DEVELOPMENT

CHAPTER 1

POVERTY AND INEQUALITY IN LATIN AMERICA

"Your servants are given no straw, yet we are told, 'Make bricks!'"

—Exodus 5:16

INTRODUCTION

Inclusive development is a development process to which all are able to contribute according to their potential, and to enjoy their fair share of the benefits of that process. The purpose of this chapter is to describe the need for more inclusive development in Latin America.

We explore poverty by examining recent Latin American data for three measures of poverty: national income, poverty lines, and poverty indexes. We explore inequality by examining recent Latin American data for two measures of inequality, the Gini Index and income ratios.

NATIONAL INCOME

For purposes of this study, the term "Latin America," is defined to be the countries of Mexico, Central America, and South America.[1]

Table 1.1 lists the countries of Latin America and indicators of their economic status.

Decentralization for Satisfying Basic Needs: An Economic Guide for Policymakers, 2nd Edition
pp. 1–15

Table 1.1. National Income

(1)	(2)	(3)	(4)	(5)	(6)
Country	*Population (2005) (millions)*	*GDP per Capita (PPP US$) (2005)*	*Growth (1990-2005)*	*Inflation (1990-2005)*	*Inflation (2004-2005)*
Argentina	38.7	14,280	1.1	7.1	9.6
Bolivia	9.2	2,819	1.3	6.3	5.4
Brazil	186.8	8,402	1.1	86.0	6.9
Chile	16.3	12,027	3.8	6.3	3.1
Colombia	44.9	7,304	0.6	15.2	5.0
Costa Rica	4.3	10,180	2.3	13.5	13.8
Ecuador	13.1	4,341	0.8	34.1	2.4
El Salvador	6.7	5,255	1.6	5.9	4.7
Guatemala	12.7	4,568	1.3	8.6	8.4
Honduras	6.8	3,430	0.5	15.0	8.8
Mexico	104.3	10,751	1.5	14.8	4.0
Nicaragua	5.5	3,674	1.8	18.9	9.4
Panama	3.2	7,605	2.2	1.0	3.3
Paraguay	5.9	4,642	–0.6	11.1	6.8
Peru	27.3	6,039	2.2	15.0	1.6
Uruguay	3.3	9,962	0.1	22.3	4.7
Venezuela	26.7	6,632	–1.0–	37.6	16.0
Latin America	515.7	7171**	1.2**	18.7**	6.7**
Medium human development	4,239.6*	20,312.6*	4.0*	n.a.	n.a.
United States	299.8	41,890	2.1	2.6	3.4

Notes: *Includes the Caribbean nations. **Average of the 17 countries listed. ***Average of the 15 countries listed for which data is available, n.a. not available.
Source: United Nations (2007/2008, Table 5, pp. 258-261, Table 14, pp. 292-295).

Population

Column (2), "Population," indicates a wide variation in country size ranging from a low of 3.2 million inhabitants in Panama to 186.8 million in Brazil. The 2005 population of Latin America (515.7 million) was almost twice that of the United States (299.8 million).

GDP and Income

Column (3) records the GDP per capita in "Purchasing Power Parity" (PPP) dollars for each country in 2005. Defining the term (see below) will show that column (3) provides estimates of national income that are comparable between countries.

Gross domestic product (GDP) is the value of all final goods and services produced in a country during a year. Since every time that someone spends $1, someone else earns $1, GDP is calculated both by measuring the expenditures for the goods and services produced and the income earned in producing them. Our focus is on the fact that GDP is a measure of national income and, in that sense, of national well-being.

GDP per capita is the total income earned in the economy divided by the population of the economy. It measures the average income per person that has been earned during a year.

PPP is a rate of exchange that accounts for price differences across countries. At the PPP US$ rate, PPP US$1 has the same purchasing power in the domestic economy as $1 has in the United States. Using this rate of exchange to calculate GDP in terms of dollars allows international comparisons (United Nations, 2007/2008, pp. 226-227).

Consequently, column (3) lists the average income per person in terms of U.S. dollars that was earned during 2005.

The table reveals sizeable differences in income across Latin American countries. The GDP per capita ranges from a low of $2,819 in Bolivia to a high of $14,280 in Argentina. Argentina's GDP per capita is over five times greater than Bolivia's.

The GDP per capita for Latin America was $7,171 in 2005. The United States' per capita GDP ($41,890) was almost six times this figure. This means that the average Latin American is living on one sixth the income of the average North American. The average Bolivian is living on about one fifteenth the income of the average North American. Latin America is a relatively poor region.

Per capita GDP hides the extent of some Latin American poverty. GDP per capita is calculated by dividing a country's total income by its population. This yields an average number that ignores the distribution of income. As we will see below, Latin America is the most unequal region of the world. Some persons receive far less than the average income while others receive far more.

Growth

Column (4) of Table 1.1 records the average annual growth rate for Latin American countries during the period 1990-2005. It is important to consider the growth rate of each country because economic growth is the most important factor contributing to poverty reduction (Nafziger, 1997, p. 125).

"Growth" measures the change in the amount of goods and services that are produced during a year. Hence, column (4) records the average annual change in each nation's purchasing power, or "real income," between 1990 and 2005.[2] Is the purchasing power of Latin Americans increasing rapidly?

Again, there is a wide variation in the performance of Latin American economies. The purchasing power of Venezuelans fell by 1% per year over the fifteen year period. The purchasing power of Chileans rose by an impressive 3.8% per year over the period.

The average growth rate in Latin America has been relatively low. The purchasing power of all Latin Americans rose by 1.2% per year during 1990-2005 compared to 4.0% for all medium human development countries and 2.1% for the United States.

Inflation

Inflation is another important measure of economic well-being. It is the percentage increase in the general level of prices. Inflation lowers the standard of living for persons with fixed incomes that do not rise with prices. The poor often live on fixed incomes. Indeed, inflation has been called "the cruelest tax on the poor."

Columns (5) and (6) of Table 1.1 list the average annual inflation rates by country for the periods 1990-2005 and 2004-2005. For the former period, inflation ranged between 1.0% (Panama) and 86.0% (Brazil). For the latter period, inflation ranged between 1.6% (Peru) and 13.8% (Argentina). Latin America's average inflation rates (18.7% and 6.7%) are far higher than those for the United States (2.6% and 3.4%). However, Latin America has succeeded in lowering its inflation over time.

Inflation is more than a tax on the poor and on others with fixed incomes. High inflation rates tend to lower growth. It is notable that the three countries with the highest inflation rates for 1990-2005 (Brazil, Venezuela, and Ecuador) had growth rates below the average growth rate for all of Latin America.

INCOME POVERTY

Columns (2) and (3) of Table 1.2 record the percentages of Latin Americans that live in "income poverty." The World Bank somewhat arbitrarily set the lines for income poverty at $1 and $2 per day in 1985 US$.[3]

Table 1.2. Income Poverty (1990-2005)*

(1)	*(2)*	*(3)*	*(4)*	*(5)*
Country	*Percent < $1 per Day***	*Percent < $2 per Day****	*Population < $1 per Day (Millions)*	*Population < $2 per Day (Millions)*
Argentina	6.6	17.4	2.55	6.73
Bolivia	23.2	42.2	2.13	3.88
Brazil	7.5	21.2	14.01	39.60
Chile	<2	5.6	n.a.	0.91
Colombia	7.0	17.8	3.14	7.99
Costa Rica	3.3	9.8	0.14	0.42
Ecuador	17.7	40.8	2.32	5.34
El Salvador	19.0	40.6	1.27	2.72
Guatemala	13.5	31.9	1.71	4.05
Honduras	14.9	35.7	1.01	2.43
Mexico	3.0	11.6	3.13	12.10
Nicaragua	45.1	79.9	2.48	4.39
Panama	7.4	18.0	0.24	0.58
Paraguay	13.6	29.8	0.80	1.76
Peru	10.5	30.6	2.87	8.35
Uruguay	<2	5.7	n.a.	0.19
Venezuela	18.5	40.1	4.94	10.71
Latin America	n.a.	n.a.	42.76	112.16
Percent of Latin America	n.a.	n.a.	8.30	21.76
Medium human development	<2/61.0****	<2/85.1****	n.a.	n.a.

Notes: *Data refer to the most recent year available during the period specified; **Poverty line is equivalent to $1.08 (1993 PPP US$); ***Poverty line is equivalent to $2.15 (1993 PPP US$); ****The low and high for all medium development countries; n.a. = not available.
Source: United Nations (2007/2008, Table 3, pp. 253-255).

The lower line is called the "extreme poverty" line and is intended to measure the income needed to attain basic nutritional needs, that is, a daily supply of 2,250 calories per person (Nafziger, 1997, p. 127). The upper poverty line provides for additional expenditures on clothing and shelter.

The percent of the population that lives on less than $1 per day ranges from a low of less than 2% in Chile and Uruguay to a shockingly high

45.1% in Nicaragua. The percent of the population that lives on less than $2 per day ranges from a low of 5.6% in Chile to an almost unimaginable 79.9% in Nicaragua. Of all medium developed countries, Nicaragua has the highest percentages of its people living below the World Bank's poverty lines.

Columns (4) and (5) use the population data of Table 1.1 to estimate the absolute numbers of people who were living on less than $1 and $2 per day in 2005. The last two rows of the table show that 42.76 million Latin Americans were living on less than $1 per day in 2005, and that this was 8.3% of the population; 112 million Latin Americans—more than 20% of the population—were living on less than $2 per day.

More than one of every five people in Latin America lives on less than $2 per day. How many more people are living on less than $3, $5, $10, $25 a day? Latin America is not the poorest region in the world, but many of its people are terribly deprived. With poverty comes suffering. This is why the World Bank wrote that "The achievement of sustained and equitable development remains the greatest challenge facing the human race" (World Bank, 1992, p. 1).

ACCESS TO BASIC GOODS AND SERVICES

A second way to measure poverty is to measure the access of people to basic goods and services. Table 1.3 provides one measure for over-all access to basic goods and services (life expectancy) and specific measures for education, health and nutrition.

All Basic Needs

Life expectancy at birth has been found to be the best single measure of over-all access to basic goods and services (Streeten, Burki, Haq, Hicks, & Stewart, 1981, p. 94). The idea is that if basic needs are met, people live a longer life. Life expectancy at birth is the number of years a newborn infant would live if prevailing patterns of age-specific mortality rates at the time of birth were to stay the same throughout the child's life (United Nations, 2007/2008, p. 368).

Life expectancy at birth ranges from a low of 64.7 years in Bolivia to a high of 78.5 years in Costa Rica. As a point of reference, life expectancy in the United States was 77.9 years in 2005. Bolivians are expected to live 13 years less than North Americans. This reflects a severely depressed access to basic goods and services in that country. Costa Rica has achieved a higher life expectancy than the United States. We could say that Chile

Table 1.3. Access to Basic Goods and Services

(1)	*(2)*	*(3)*	*(4)*	*(5)*
Country	*Life Expectancy at Birth (Years) 2005*	*Net Primary Enrolment Ratio (%) 2005*	*Infant Mortality Rate (Per 1,000 Live Births, 2005)*	*Children Under Weight for Age (% Under Age 5 1996-2005)*
Argentina	74.8	99	15	4
Bolivia	64.7	95	52	8
Brazil	71.1	95	31	6
Chile	78.3	90	8	1
Colombia	72.3	87	17	7
Costa Rica	78.5	n.a.	11	5
Ecuador	74.7	98	22	12
El Salvador	71.3	93	23	10
Guatemala	69.7	94	32	23
Honduras	69.4	91	31	17
Mexico	75.6	98	22	8
Nicaragua	71.9	87	30	10
Panama	75.1	98	19	8
Paraguay	71.3	88	20	5
Peru	70.7	96	23	8
Uruguay	75.9	93	14	5
Venezuela	73.2	91	18	5
Average Latin America	72.8**	95**	26**	8.3*
United States	77.9	92	6	n.a.

Notes: *Average for the 17 countries listed for which data is available. **Includes Caribbean Nations, n.a.= not available.
Source: United Nations (2007/2008, Table 1, pp. 244-247, Table 3, pp. 254-257, Table 12 pp. 284-287.

"has arrived" except for its high level of inequality to be considered below. High inequality implies that many persons are deprived of basic necessities and live a shorter life.

The average life expectancy for Latin America is 72.8 years. This is 5.1 years shorter than the life expectancy of the United States (77.9) signifying a relatively low level of achievement in satisfying basic needs.

Education

The net primary enrolment ratio is the ratio of enrolled children of primary school age to the total population of that age (United Nations, 2004, p. 179). Primary education provides the basic elements of education at such establishments as primary and elementary schools (United Nations, 2007/2008, p. 365).

Nicaragua and Colombia have the lowest net primary enrolment ratio in Latin America, 87%. In these countries, more than 1 of every 10 children of elementary school age is not in school.

The data indicate that the average Latin American country has achieved a higher net primary enrolment ratio (95%) than the United States (92%). The high achievement in Latin America may arise partly from data errors, but it also reflects recent efforts to improve educational outcomes. This is to be applauded. However, the concept of the enrolment ratio ignores significant differences in quality between the schools of the two regions. Latin American schools are more often overcrowded, lacking materials, staffed with poorly trained teachers, lacking technology, and so on.

Health

The infant mortality rate is the probability of dying between birth and one year of age, expressed per 1,000 live births (United Nations, 2007/2008, p. 368). It is a sign of poor health, not only of the infants, but also of the mothers who bore them. The average infant mortality rate for Latin America is more than four times that of the United States.

Nutrition

The term, "children under age 5 who are underweight for their age," includes both moderately and severely underweight children. Moderate underweight is defined as more than two standard deviations below the median weight for the age group. Severe underweight is defined as more than three standard deviations below the median weight.

In the average Latin American country, almost 10% of the children under age 5 are underweight. In the worst case—Guatemala—one in every four children are underweight. Malnourished children have difficulty learning. Undernourishment at a young age is known to have detrimental effects on the health of a person throughout his or her life (Skoufias, 2001, p. 59).

Table 1.4. Human Development Index (HDI)

(1) Country	(2) HDI 2005	(3) HDI 1990	(4) HDI Improvement (1990-2002)
Argentina	0.869	0.810	0.059
Bolivia	0.695	0.603	0.092
Brazil	0.800	0.714	0.086
Chile	0.867	0.784	0.083
Colombia	0.791	0.727	0.064
Costa Rica	0.846	0.791	0.055
Ecuador	0.772	0.710	0.062
El Salvador	0.735	0.648	0.087
Guatemala	0.689	0.583	0.106
Honduras	0.700	0.624	0.076
Mexico	0.829	0.761	0.068
Nicaragua	0.710	0.589	0.121
Panama	0.812	0.748	0.064
Paraguay	0.755	0.719	0.036
Peru	0.773	0.706	0.073
Uruguay	0.852	0.803	0.049
Venezuela	0.792	0.759	0.033
Average Latin America*	0.782	0.710	0.072
United States	0.951	0.914	0.037

Note: *Average for the 17 countries listed.
Source: United Nations (2007/2008, Table 1, pp. 244-247, Table 2, pp. 249-252)

POVERTY INDEX

Table 1.4 measures poverty by using a composite index, the Human Development Index. An index is a summary measure of poverty that incorporates several characteristics that make a person poor.

Column (2) records the Human Development Index (HDI) of Latin American countries for the year 2005. The HDI is calculated by the United Nations Development Program (United Nations, 2007/2008, pp. 355-356). It measures achievement in three basic dimensions of human development—a long and healthy life as measured by life expectancy at birth; knowledge as measured by the adult literacy rate and school enrolment; and a decent standard of living, as measured by GDP per capita. The HDI can range between 0 and 1; higher values represent a higher level of development.

There is substantial variation in human development between the countries. The HDI ranges from a low of 0.689 in Guatemala to a high of 0.869 in Argentina, a difference of 18 points. Bolivia, Guatemala, and Honduras are the worst performers, having HDIs at 0.70 or less. Nicaragua's HDI is only slightly higher at 0.710.

The average HDI for Latin America (0.782) is substantially lower than the HDI for the United States (0.951). This difference of 17 points means that many Latin Americans live substantially shorter and less healthy lives, are relatively uneducated, and have a substantially lower standard of living than the people of the United States.

Column (3) shows the human development indexes for 1990 and column (4) measures the difference in the indexes between 1990 and 2005. All countries made some progress in human development between 1990 and 2005. The progress ranges from a high of 0.121 in Nicaragua to a low of 0.033 in Venezuela. It is good that progress has been made. However, Latin America clearly has a very long way to go, and continued progress is extremely important.

INEQUALITY

The Gini index is a number that measures the extent to which the distribution of income (or consumption) among individuals or households within a country deviates from a perfectly equal distribution (United Nations, 2007/2008, 366).

Figure 1.1 illustrates the derivation and meaning of the Gini index. The cumulative percentage of the population is measured on the horizontal axis, starting with the poorest at the left and moving to the richest at the right. The cumulative percentage of total income received is measured on the vertical axis.

The diagonal straight line is the "line of perfect equality." Assume that there are 10 people in the economy and a total income of $10. If income is distributed equally, 5 persons have $5; therefore, 50% of the population receives 50% of the income. Whatever the number of persons, X percent of the population receives the same X percent of the income, and the distribution is represented by some point on the line of perfect equality.

The curve is the "Lorenz Curve" that represents the actual distribution of income. In 2002, the poorest 20% of Bolivia's population received 1.5% of the country's income (United Nations, 2007/2008, Table 15, p. 283).

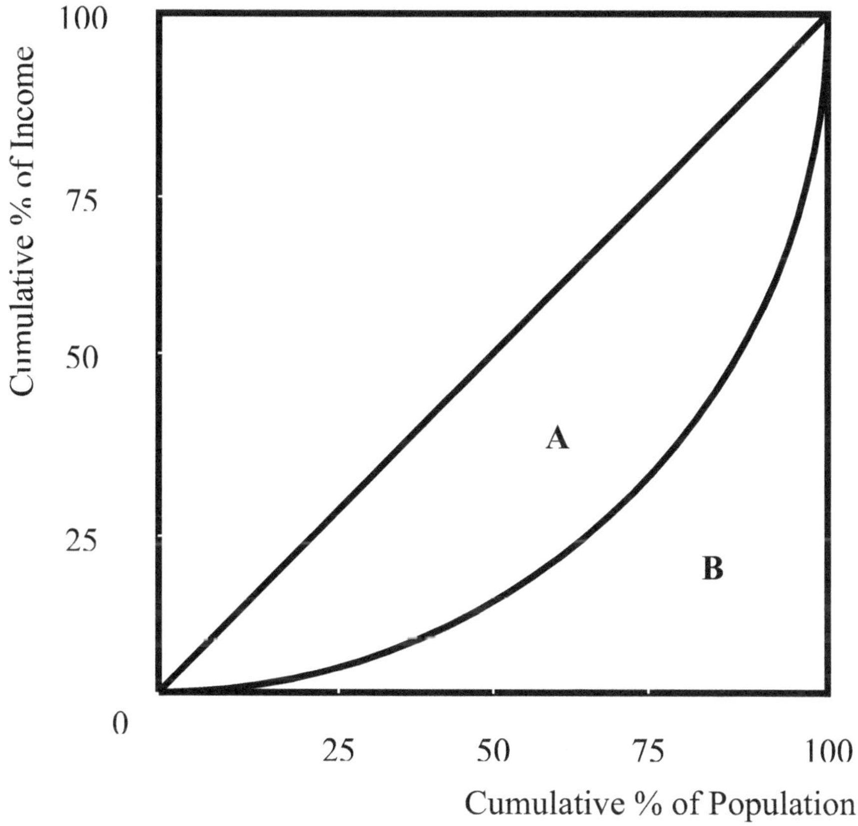

Source: McConnell, Brue, and Flynn (2009).

Figure 1.1. Lorenz Curve.

This means its Lorenz Curve lies far below the line of perfect equality. In general, the greater the inequality the lower the Lorenz Curve.

The Gini index measures inequality by dividing area A between the Lorenz Curve and the line of perfect equality by the area $(A + B)$ and multiplying by 100 (Gini $= A/(A+B) \times 100$).

If there is perfect equality, the Lorenz Curve is identical to the line of perfect equality, and so area A equals zero, and the Gini index equals zero. If there is perfect *inequality*, the Lorenz Curve coincides with the horizontal axis and the vertical axis on the right. Here, B equals zero, and so area A equals area $(A + B)$, and the Gini index equals 100.

To summarize, if there is perfect equality, the Gini index equals 0; if there is perfect inequality, the Gini index equals 100. The higher the Gini index, the higher the inequality.

Inequality Within Latin America

Column (3) of Table 1.5 shows the Gini indexes for Latin America for the years recorded in column (2). Comparison of the values of the index for different countries indicates that inequality within the region is

Table 1.5. Inequality

(1)	*(2)*	*(3)*	*(4)*	*(5)*
Country	*Survey Year*	*Gini Index*	*Richest 10% to Poorest 10%*	*Richest 20% to Poorest 20%*
Argentina	2004	51.3	40.9	17.8
Bolivia	2002	60.1	168.1	42.3
Brazil	2004	57.0	51.3	21.8
Chile	2003	54.9	33.0	15.7
Colombia	2003	58.6	63.8	25.3
Costa Rica	2003	49.8	37.8	15.6
Ecuador	1998	53.6	44.9	17.3
El Salvador	2002	52.4	57.5	20.9
Guatemala	2002	55.1	48.2	20.3
Honduras	2003	53.8	34.2	17.2
Mexico	2004	46.1	24.6	12.8
Nicaragua	2001	43.1	15.5	8.8
Panama	2003	56.1	57.5	23.9
Paraguay	2003	58.4	65.4	25.7
Peru	2003	52.0	30.4	15.2
Uruguay	2003	44.9	17.9	10.2
Venezuela	2003	48.2	48.3	16.0
Average Latin America	n.a.	52.7	49.4	19.2
United States	2000	40.8	15.9	8.4
Japan	1993	24.9	4.5	3.4

Note: n.a. = not applicable
Source: United Nations (2007/2008, Table 15, pp. 296-299).

diverse. The indexes range from a low of 43.1 in Nicaragua to a high of 60.1 in Bolivia. Bolivia's index is 40% higher than Nicaragua's.

Column (4) presents another measure of inequality within the region: the ratio of the amount of income received by the richest 10% to that received by the poorest 10%. In Brazil, the richest 10% of the population receives a whopping 168.1 times more income than the poorest 10%. In the average Latin American country, the richest 10% receives 49.4 times more income than the poorest 10%.

Column (5) shows that the 20% ratios are less extreme than the 10% ratios. This indicates that income is heavily concentrated in the hands of a small number of people.

Most Unequal Region

Latin America's inequality is high relative to other regions of the world. In Table 1.5, the average Gini index for Latin America (52.7) is about 12 points higher than the Gini index for the United States (40.8), the most unequal industrialized country. More telling, Latin America's average Gini index (52.7) is almost 28 points higher than Japan's Gini index (24.9).

Similarly, Latin America's income ratios are much higher than the ratios for the United States and Japan. In the 10% category, the average for Latin America (49.4) is over 3 times higher than the ratio for the United States (15.9) and 11 times higher than Japan's ratio (4.5).

The literature concludes that Latin America is the most unequal region in the world. Londoño finds that for a sample of 102 countries, the average Latin American country has a Gini index 4.1 points higher than countries with similar per capita income. He estimated a Gini index of 56 for the region as a whole, which is higher than Yotopoulos's estimate for all the developing world (50.1), and higher than the expected level for Latin America's level of development (50) (Londoño, 1996, pp. 3-4). Similarly, a study by Székely and Hilgert concluded that Latin America has the "highest regional Gini in the world" (Székely & Hilgert, cited in Franko, 2003, p. 355).

John Scott makes the following comparison of Gini indexes between regions of the world for 1990 (Scott, 2001, Table 1.4.1, p. 14). The Gini indexes are population-weighted averages. The Gini index for the Latin American region is close to 20 points above the average for both low- and high-income countries.

There are many social, political and economic implications of extreme inequality. One important economic implication is that inequality indicates the depth of poverty in Latin America. Average incomes (per capita GDPs)

Table 1.6. Average Inequality in International Regions (1990)

Region	*Gini*
LAC	55.4
Sub-Saharan Africa	45.0
East Asia and Pacific	41.2
Middle East and North Africa	35.6
South Asia	29.8
Eastern Europe (unweighted)	28.9
Lower income	36.8
Lower-middle income	44.4
Upper-middle income	56.4
High-income economies	34.5

are much lower in Latin America than in the United States. However, the extreme inequality means that the low average incomes hide the depth of poverty that really exists. There are many people with very much less income than the average. And many poor fall far below the poverty lines.

CONCLUSION

Latin America is poor and unequal. Latin America's per capita income is only about one sixth that of the United States. About 20% of Latin Americans live on less than $2 per day. The life expectancy of the average Latin American is 5 years less than the life expectance of the average person of the United States. Latin America's HDI is 17 points lower than that of the United States. The average Gini index for the region is 29% higher than the United States' Gini, and more than 110% higher than Japan's.

The effect of poverty and inequality is not only the misery of the poor. It excludes the poor from full participation in the production process and its benefits. Human resources are wasted. Not only inequity, but also inefficiency abound. The economy stagnates, and almost everyone suffers.

The solution is an equitable form of development in which everyone participates according to his or her potential. In chapter 2, the path to inclusive development is explored. Succeeding chapters explore the role of decentralization in achieving it.

NOTES

1. Caribbean countries are sometimes included in the term, "Latin America." The Caribbean countries are Antigua and Barbuda, Bahamas, Barbados,

Belize, Cuba, Dominica, Dominican Republic, Grenada, Guyana, Haiti, Jamaica, Saint Kitts and Nevis, Saint Lucia, Saint Vincent and the Grenadines, Suriname, Trinidad and Tobago.

2. The World Bank Atlas method of calculating exchange rates used to convert currencies into U.S. dollars takes inflation into account.
3. The current poverty line for each country is found by converting the dollars into local currency using the Summers-Heston Purchasing Power Parity (PPP) exchange rates. A local consumer price index is then used to derive the poverty line for years other than 1985. This procedure gives the amount of money required in each country to buy the same commodities that in turn makes the Bank poverty estimates comparable across countries (Morley, 1995, p. 37).

CHAPTER 2

INCLUSIVE DEVELOPMENT THROUGH SATISFYING BASIC NEEDS

"The greatest challenge facing humanity is sustained and equitable development"

—World Development Report (World Bank, 1992).

INTRODUCTION

In chapter 1, Latin America's poverty and inequality were described. Poverty and inequality are not only a social problem. They are also an economic problem. A vast number of the most valuable resource—humans—are being excluded from the development process and its benefits. Human resources are wasted. The result is not only misery, but also economic stagnation. With stagnation, almost everyone is affected negatively.

The purpose of this chapter is to help plot a course for eliminating poverty and extreme inequality, and for enhancing economic growth. An essential part of that course is the satisfaction of everybody's basic needs for education, health, nutrition, and other essential goods and services within a short period of time. This is a key to enabling *all* people to con-

Decentralization for Satisfying Basic Needs: An Economic Guide for Policymakers, 2nd Edition
pp. 17–23

tribute to the development process according to their potential, and to benefit from the process.

The first part of the chapter describes what is called the basic needs approach to development. We define the objective of the approach, the means to achieve it, and the rationale that justifies it. Next, we examine empirical evidence in support of the hypothesis that satisfying basic needs enhances economic growth. Finally, we discuss the feasibility of satisfying basic needs by examining the cost of doing so.

THE BASIC NEEDS APPROACH TO DEVELOPMENT

The objective of a basic needs approach to development is a full life *for all*. The means of achieving the objective is to satisfy the basic needs of all people within a short period of time. This renders the least privileged more productive and more able to contribute to the production process. They are freed to earn higher incomes and to make the other choices necessary to live a full life.

What do we mean by "basic needs"? A standard list contains basic education, health services, nutrition, housing, water and sanitation (Streeten, Burki, Haq, Hicks, & Stewart, 1981, p. vii). The rationale is exceedingly simple. An educated person is more productive and able to earn a higher income. Healthy people do not miss work. Nourished people have more energy. Clean water, housing and sanitation make people more healthy, more able to learn and more productive.

The list is not an automatic cure-all. Rather, it is a working list that includes goods and services that are essential for including people in the development process. However, the needs of each community must be analyzed, and the list should be expanded or contracted as the circumstances demand. A rural community, for example, may have clean water, but may require a road in order to transport its agricultural produce to market.

Nobel Prize winner Amartya Sen and his colleague Jean Dréze have elaborated the requirements for instituting an inclusive development process. They define development as more than the satisfaction of basic needs. They define it broadly as "the expansion of the real freedoms that the citizens enjoy to pursue the objectives they have reason to value" (Dréze & Sen, 1995, p. 10). In short, development is the freedom to be and to do. Poverty, in this view, is not merely an impoverished state in which the person lives, but also the lack of freedom to choose other types of living such as the freedom to find productive and remunerative employment, the freedom to participate fully in the social and political life of the community, and so on.

Having defined development broadly, Dréze and Sen find many means to achieve it. One is the growth of gross national product (GNP), but the impact of GNP growth on human freedom can be extremely variable depending on the nature of that growth. For example, the impact depends on how employment-intensive the growth is, and whether the gains are channeled into remedying the deprivations of the neediest. Other means to development include investment in physical capital, new technology, the development of financial institutions, and macroeconomic policy that generates full employment without inflation. The insights of Drèze and Sen by no means negate the importance of satisfying the basic needs. Rather, they show that satisfying basic needs is a *necessary,* but not *sufficient*, condition for establishing an inclusive development process that benefits all.

Drèze and Sen find that satisfying basic needs is essential for achieving development in at least five ways (Dréze & Sen, 1995, pp. 14-15). First, basic goods and services have *intrinsic importance*, i.e., they are valuable in themselves and contribute directly to a person's effective freedom (quality of life). Second, they have *instrumental personal roles* in that they can help a person do many things such as getting a job. Third, they have *instrumental social roles*, in that they can facilitate public discussion of social needs and encourage informed collective demands. Fourth, they have *instrumental process roles* such as reducing child labor and broadening the horizon of children, especially girls. Fifth, they have *empowerment and distributive roles* that enable disadvantaged groups to resist oppression, to organize politically, and to get a more fair deal. Thus, while Drèze and Sen broaden the basic needs approach to development, they reaffirm the importance of satisfying simple basic needs such as education, health and nutrition.

Basic Needs and Growth

Does satisfying basic needs speed growth or does it slow it? A priori reasoning might lead one to answer the question either way. Satisfying basic needs tends to speed growth because it makes people more productive. It might slow growth because, for example, spending money on satisfying basic needs reduces the amount of money available for the purchase of machinery and other forms of physical capital. Empirical evidence is required to answer the question.

Empirical Evidence

Norman Hicks, an economist of the World Bank, studied the relation between the satisfaction of basic needs and the growth of 83 developing countries. He found that the 12 countries that had an above average success in satisfying basic needs in 1960 had a relatively high growth rate in the following period, 1960-1977. The average annual growth rate in the real gross national product for all 83 countries during 1960-1977 was 2.4%. But the average growth rate for the countries that had above average success in satisfying basic needs was 5.7%. The countries that had satisfied more basic needs grew almost 2.5 times faster than the other countries. Hicks concludes that "a higher level of basic-needs satisfaction appears to lead to higher growth rates in the future" (Hicks, 1979, p. 992).

Amartya Sen and Jean Dréze compared the satisfaction of basic needs and the growth records of China and India. China's government implemented a large basic needs program for ideological reasons before turning to the market system, whereas India did not. Remember that the best single indicator of having met basic needs is life expectancy. In 1981, the life expectancy at birth in China was 67.7 years, while in India it was a much lower 53.9 years. China had supplied the basic services that prolong life while India had not.

This relatively high satisfaction of basic needs, according to Sen and Dréze, prepared China to dramatically increase production, once the country adopted the market system. Therefore, during the period following 1981 (1980-1992), the average annual growth rate of GDP in China was 9.1% while less-prepared India grew at a much lower rate of 5.2%. "The 'magic' of the China market rests on the solid foundations of social changes that had occurred earlier" (Drèze & Sen, 1995, p. 74).

In a similar vein, Sen and Dréze argue that the amazing growth record of the "Four Tigers (South Korea, Hong Kong, Singapore, Taiwan) is due in part to their having expanded education. "Because these countries attained universal primary education early, literacy was high and cognitive skill levels were substantially above those in other developing economies. Firms therefore had an easier time upgrading the skills of their workers and mastering new technology" (Drèze & Sen, 1995, p. 74).

This is convincing evidence that satisfying basic needs does not detract from growth, but rather contributes to it. If so, the traditional thinking about satisfying basic needs is turned upside down. Supplying basic education to children is not a welfare program that impoverishes the country. Instead, it is a development program that enriches the country. Satisfying basic needs reduces suffering, and that is good. But it is also a development policy. Better still, it is an *inclusive* development policy that tends to benefit everybody.

Basic Needs and Efficiency

The basic needs approach to development also revolutionizes thinking about efficiency. Satisfying basic needs is not a redistribution program that interferes with efficiency. Instead, it enhances efficiency by enhancing the productivity of people who had been excluded from full participation in the development process. It activates previously unemployed or under-employed resources. Satisfying basic needs is not primarily a welfare program, but rather a development strategy.

Basic Education and Growth

George Psacharopoulos estimated the social rates of return to basic education in a 1994 study. The rates of return were found by calculating the discount rates that equated a stream of education benefits to a stream of educational costs at a given point in time. Benefits consisted of increased earnings. The costs included not only private expenditures for school materials and such, but also the foregone earnings of students, and government expenditures for education.

After reviewing all of the studies that he could find, the author concluded that the average social rate of return to primary education in Latin America and the Caribbean was 18%. Interestingly, the returns to secondary and higher education were lower: 12.8% and 12.3%, respectively (Psacharopoulos, 1994, Table 1, p. 1328). He concluded that "investment in education continues to be a very attractive investment opportunity in the world today" (Psacharopoulos, 1994, p. 1325).

Furthermore, he found that the social returns to primary education were highest in the poorest countries. The returns to primary education in low income countries ($610 or less) were 23.4%. The social return to lower-middle-income countries (to $2,449) was 18.2%. The return to upper-middle-income countries (to $7,619) was 14.3% (Psacharopoulos, 1994, Table 2, p. 1328).

These high returns reflect increased productivity. Increased incomes follow increased production. One additional year of schooling in Thailand was found to add about 2.5% to farm output (Psacharopoulos, 1994, p. 1328). An additional year of schooling in East Asia contributed over 3% to GDP.

Another interesting conclusion is that the returns to investment in education declined over a 15-year period (1970-1985). The declines in the returns to primary, secondary and higher education were 8.2%, 5.7% and 1.7% respectively (Psacharopoulos, 1994, Table 5, p. 1329).

John B. Knight and his colleagues help to explain the declines (Knight et al., 1992). They argue that in the 1960s and 1970s, primary graduates were in scarce supply, so that a primary-school certificate was a passport to a white-collar job. In the 1990s, however, after decades of rapid educational expansion and the displacement of primary graduates by secondary graduates, primary completers are fortunate to get even the most menial blue-collar wage job. This suggests a growing need to continue support for education through at least the secondary level.

The Low Cost of Satisfying Basic Needs

Measuring the cost of satisfying basic needs is not without difficulties. Costs vary by country. And the marginal cost of satisfying the basic needs of additional persons may be different from the average cost of satisfying basic needs of all those in the past. For example, children not in school might be harder to induce to come to school because of a greater need for them to contribute income to the family, or because they live in more remote areas. Another difficulty is that since basic needs are interdependent, the cost of satisfying one basic need influences the cost of satisfying others. For example, education promotes better health and reduces the cost of providing basic health services. Finally, it is difficult to estimate the future development and the participation of labor in that development. If they are high, both the level of unmet needs and the cost of satisfying them fall.

Around the year 2000, UNICEF estimated a shortfall in public spending of up to $80 billion a year (1995 dollars) to achieve universal provision of basic services, with around $206-216 billion required and only $136 billion presently being spent (United Nations, 2000, Box 4.5, 79). This shortfall is twice the $40 billion cost that was estimated at the time of the World Summit for Social Development in 1995. Let us assume that the high figure is correct. Can we afford to pay it?

Allowing for inflation, the cost of satisfying basic needs would rise to $115 billion in 2007.[1] In 2007, the GDP of the United States was $13,808 billion (Bureau of Economic Analysis, 2009a). In the same year, the GDP of all OECD countries was $38,728 billion (OECD, 2008a). The estimated $115 billion cost of satisfying basic needs is less than 1% (0.83%) of the U.S. GDP, and it is only 0.3% of the GDP of OECD countries.

World military spending is conservatively estimated to be $1,100 billion for 2007 (World Wide Military Expenditures, 2009). $80 billion equals 7.3% of this spending. If the world would redirect 7.3% of its military spending, all basic needs could be satisfied. By how much would the need for military spending fall if the basic needs of all people were satisfied?

Nobel Prize winner Joseph Stiglitz and Linda Bilmes estimate that the total cost of the Iraq war will exceed $3 trillion (Stiglitz & Bilmes, 2008). This is sufficient money to assure the satisfaction of basic needs of everyone on earth for more than 25 years.

Norman Hicks states that the resources for satisfying basic needs can be found by redirecting consumption expenditures of both the poor and the rich away from non-basic-needs expenditures, and from unnecessary or even wasteful public-sector expenditures (Hicks, 1979, p. 985).

CONCLUSION

The satisfaction of basic needs is an effective approach to development. It increases span of life, giving people more years to contribute to the economy. It increases the rate of growth by making people more productive. The cost is low, making it an excellent investment. It eliminates the inefficient waste of human resources by empowering them to realize their potential and to contribute.

The policy should be to satisfy the basic needs of all people within a short period of time. But how does a country implement a basic needs approach to development? Chapter 3 uses a Service Delivery Framework to help answer this question.

NOTE

1. The additional cost of satisfying basic needs in 2007 was estimated using the price index for the gross domestic product of the United States (BEA, 2009).

PART II

MODEL OF DECENTRALIZATION

CHAPTER 3

EFFECTIVE SERVICE DELIVERY

"Education is a way to get out of poverty."

—Indigent Person of Ecuador

INTRODUCTION

Chapter 1 described the widespread poverty and extreme inequality that characterize Latin America. Chapter 2 introduced the basic needs approach to development. The objective of this development strategy is to satisfy within a short period of time all basic needs that render the poor productive and that empower them to live a full life. We saw that doing so is not merely a humanitarian welfare program, but also an effective means of development. It benefits not only the poor, but also the nation.

The purpose of this chapter is to present a model that identifies the key agents and that describes their roles in satisfying basic needs effectively. The framework focuses on the public sector since it necessarily plays a dominant role in satisfying basic needs. In chapter 4, the model is expanded to identify the elements of successful decentralization. The expanded decentralization model is, in turn, used to understand and evaluate decentralization programs oriented toward satisfying the basic needs of the poor.

The service delivery framework is derived from economic theory and from the experience of the World Bank. It is heavily dependent on *World*

Decentralization for Satisfying Basic Needs: An Economic Guide for Policymakers, 2nd Edition
pp. 25–39

Development Report 2004 (World Bank, 2003, Chapters 3-6), and on earlier works by Paul Streeten and associates (Streeten, Burki, Haq, Hicks, & Stewart, 1981) and Frances Stewart (Stewart, 1985).

The chapter is divided into four sections. After briefly arguing that the public sector plays the dominate role in satisfying basic needs, the second section identifies the principle agents in satisfying the basic needs of the poor. The third section describes the ideal role of each agent. The chapter concludes with a checklist for policymakers and some concluding remarks.

ROLE OF PUBLIC SECTOR

The public sector necessarily plays a large role in delivering basic goods and services to the poor. Economic theory provides two sound reasons for service delivery by the government: private market failure and equity.

Private Market Failure

Private markets sometimes fail to provide the quantity of basic goods and services that maximize society's welfare. One important case is that of external benefits, that is, benefits that are received by others than the buyer of a good or service. Basic education, for example, benefits others than the graduate partly because it increases productivity and thereby lowers prices of the product produced by the graduate for everybody. But in demanding education, the student only considers the benefit to himself. Hence, demand is below the level that maximizes social welfare.

"Public goods" (goods that, once produced, cannot be denied to nonpayers else and whose consumption does not diminish consumption by others) are an extreme form of market failure. Mosquito control in a malaria endemic area is an example. Everyone benefits from mosquito control regardless of whether he or she helps to pay for it. Consequently, the smart thing to do is to remain silent about one's willingness to pay for it. Silence means that the demand for mosquito control collapses. Without demand, the private market fails to provide the control, even though society would be better off with it.

Private market failure can also arise from imperfect information. A lack of knowledge about the benefits of education can lead to students demanding less than the optimum amount of schooling.

The failure of private markets to give the best amount of a basic good or service calls for government intervention to correct the undersupply. The intervention may come in the form of government provision through public enterprises, or the government may contract out production to private enterprises. Other options are to subsidize consumers or disseminate information on the benefits of consuming basic goods and services.

Equity

The second economic justification for government intervention is equity. Economic theory shows that private competitive markets automatically allocate resources efficiently in the sense that they generate the welfare-maximizing quantity of each good and service (McConnell, Brue, & Flynn, 2009, p. 28).

However, there is a very important *caveat* to this assertion. Free and perfect markets automatically generate the welfare-maximizing quantity of each good and service, but there is no market mechanism that automatically generates the distribution of income that maximizes social satisfaction.

The problem is that there is a different demand and a different efficient market quantity for each distribution of income. But each efficient market quantity is not equally satisfying. If all income is distributed equally, there is a demand for each good and service, and the free market generates the quantity of each product or service that maximizes social satisfaction—*for that distribution of income*. If, on the other hand, one person has all the income, there is a different demand and a different efficient outcome. But obviously, the two efficient outcomes do not yield the same satisfaction to society.

There is no market mechanism that compensates for chance inheritances, place of birth, parents, health, accidents, discovery of oil, and so on, all of which arbitrarily influence the distribution of income and social welfare. Latin America is an extremely unequal region primarily because the Spanish conquest distributed most of the resources to a few *conquistadores*. Good judgment (and that is all that we have) seems to indicate that this extreme inequality is not in the best interest of society. Who is to correct it? There is only one agent capable of doing so—the government. One way to correct it is to tax the wealthy and use the revenues to supply capacitating goods and services to the poor.

MODEL OF EFFECTIVE SERVICE DELIVERY

Figure 3.1 presents a general framework for delivery by the public sector of basic goods and services to the poor. The figure shows that three agents are primarily responsible for satisfying the basic needs of the poor:

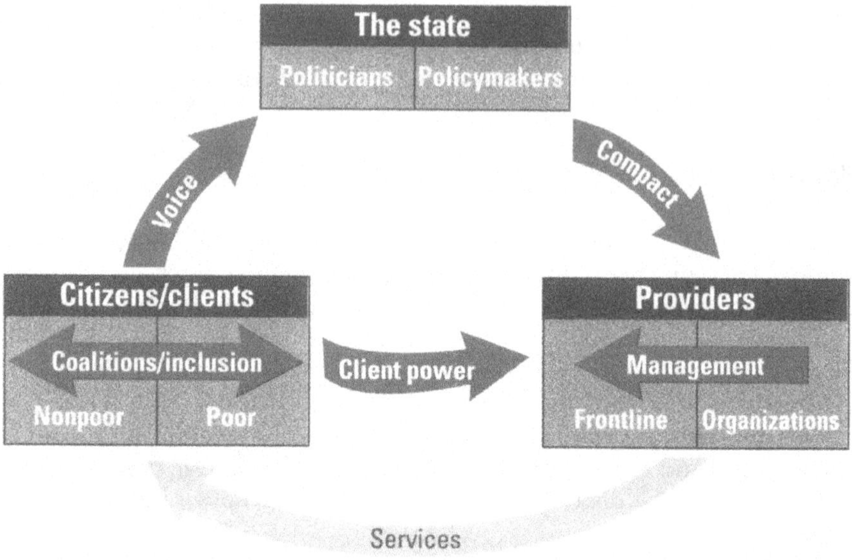

Source: World Bank (2003, p. 49).

Figure 3.1. Service delivery model.

citizens, the *state* and *providers*. These agents interrelate through three relationships: *voice*, *compact* and *client power.*

The Agents

Citizens/Clients

Webster's dictionary defines citizens as members of a nation who owe allegiance to the government and are entitled to the nation's protection and privileges (Random House, 1991, p. 248). Citizens are also the clients of the organizations that provide the basic goods and services supplied by government. Citizens/clients consist of both the poor and the nonpoor.

Politicians/Policymakers

The second agent, the state, refers to the government. The government may be federal, state, or local. The government consists of Politicians and policymakers. The politicians are the presidents, the governors and the mayors. They discharge the fundamental responsibilities of the state to legislate, to regulate and to tax.

The other government agent, the policymakers, set the fundamental rules by which the service providers are to operate. They determine the beneficiaries, they enforce standards, and they determine the conditions under which providers receive public funds. In many cases, the policymaker is the legislature or a central ministry such as the ministry of education.

Providers

The third key agent in service delivery is the provider. Providers are responsible for delivering basic goods and services to the people. Providers consist of organizations and frontline providers. A provider organization can be a public organization, whatever the name—ministry, department, agency, or bureau. It can also be an autonomous public enterprise such as a public hospital. It can be large (public sector ministries with tens of thousands of teachers) or small (a single community-run primary school). The frontline provider is the person who comes into direct contact with clients—teachers, doctors, nurses, and so on.

Three Key Relationships

Voice

Effective service delivery to the poor begins with poor citizens "voicing" their needs to the state. The poor may voice their preferences to politicians through both formal political mechanisms such as political parties and voting, or informal ones such as advocacy groups and public information campaigns. Advocacy groups may be NGOs (nongovernmental organizations), or they may be coalitions of both the poor and the nonpoor. Whatever the mechanism, effective service delivery begins with poor citizens voicing their needs to the state.

Economic theory shows that in the private sector, economic well-being is maximized by consumers demanding and by businesses responding to that demand (McConnell et al., 2009, pp. 128–129). The idea is that consumers know best what they want and need. The main function of business is to read consumer demand, to supply the goods and services that consumers are willing and able to buy, and to charge the free market price necessary to cover the costs of production. This "consumer sovereignty" leads to much more satisfying results than having goods and services pushed onto buyers through force or trickery. Business sovereignty leads to exploitation and a loss of social welfare.

The concept of voice transfers consumer sovereignty to the public sector. "Citizen sovereignty" is beneficial to citizens just as consumer sovereignty is advantageous to consumers in the private sector (Musgrave & Musgrave, 1989, chapter 4). The ideal role of citizens is to demand public goods and services from the government. The role of government is to read that demand, to supply the public goods and services demanded, and to pay the costs of doing so by taxing the citizenry. The most effective way to tax is considered in chapters 8 and 9. Citizen sovereignty is generally much better than having politicians ignore citizen input and decide "from on high" which public goods and services citizens ought to consume.

What remains if the poor are voiceless? Passivity? Patronage? Domination? Neglect? Perpetual poverty? If, on the other hand, the voice of the poor is strong, the poor become subjects of their own destiny rather than passive objects of poverty programs (such as they may be). The poor become participants in their own development as well as in the development of the nation. Surely voice increases the likelihood that poverty programs succeed and speeds the pace of development.

This is not to say that citizen voice is the only determinant of objectives. One must also introduce the findings of science into policymaking. For example, scientific empirical studies show that basic education is an effective means of increasing incomes. Poor citizens delegate to government the power to take these studies into account as well as the power to work out other policy details.

The model proposes citizen sovereignty, but in fact poor citizens are often (if not usually) voiceless. How does this happen, especially in a region in which the majority of people are poor?

The poor may be afraid to voice their needs because doing so can impose large costs on them when their interests clash with those in authority. In a visit to Mexico, the author interviewed two destitute families who made their living by scavenging in a Mexico City garbage dump. They received no public services, except that their makeshift houses were located on publicly owned land. They were very hesitant to speak of their needs for fear that they would be displaced. As we were leaving, they ran after us. They had spoken somewhat freely and were in a state of panic. They feared that they had voiced something that would cause them to be displaced from the public land that they were occupying.

Voice may be limited by imperfections in the political process. Elites may control the government and be indifferent to the plight of poor people. Voters may lack information about the role their elected representatives play in affecting the quantity and quality of public goods and services. Voters may be easily swayed by political propaganda, or they may vote on the basis of a candidate's charisma or ethnic identity rather than record. Voters may be swayed by bribes. Special interest groups may capture policies by providing campaign finance or mobilizing votes. Social polarization can lead to voting based on social, ethnic, or religious identity rather than policy or service delivery performance. Politicians may be unwilling to commit to supplying basic goods and services such as education because their term in office is too short to claim credit for policies with long maturing outcomes; promises of jobs or public works projects that can be delivered soon after an election may be much more effective in winning an election.

Hence, a key policy objective must be to strengthen the voice of the poor where it is weak. The voice of the poor can be increased in many ways: increasing the participation of the poor in elections, generating information on the record of incumbents and background on election candidates, making government budgets accessible to citizens, village level participatory audits of local public expenditures, citizen report cards in which the performance of politicians in supplying basic goods and services is graded, improving the law, and knowledge sharing coalitions that include both the poor and the nonpoor, In the next chapter, we will see that one of the main objectives of decentralization is to strengthen citizen voice by bringing services and elected politicians closer to the citizen/client.

The relationship of voice includes enforcing the findings of monitoring. If monitoring is decentralized to clients (see below), voters need verify only that politicians have made resources available for schools, clinics and other basic goods and services to decide whether to reward or punish them at election time. Easy access to budgets helps voters to make their decisions. Monitoring is discussed more fully below under client power.

Compact

The state begins to respond to citizen demand through the second type of relationship, the compact between the government and the provider of basic goods and services. The compact is a broad agreement between the policymaker and the provider that is to guide the delivery of the goods and services. It embodies a broad plan and policy for satisfying basic needs. What are the elements of an ideal compact?

Objectives and Sectors

The first step in forming a compact is to determine program objectives. The general objective is, of course, to enhance the productivity of all the poor in a short period of time in order to empower them to produce, to earn, and to live full lives. The compact may also identify somewhat more specific objectives such as prioritizing help for the *rural* poor (who are often most impoverished). The determination of objectives should be heavily influenced by citizen voice.

The second step is to choose basic needs sectors in accord with their ability to meet the objectives. Again, citizen voice should influence the selection of sectors. If it is found, for example, that the productivity of the rural poor is being hindered by an inability to read, one sector to be chosen would be basic education for the rural poor.

In selecting sectors, it is important to consider linkages and phasing. Sick and hungry children cannot learn. Consequently, it may be necessary to complement the education program with health services and nutrition supplements. Providing "packages" of services is absolutely necessary to avoid having complementary needs undermine the effectiveness of the basic needs program.

Phasing refers to choosing the most effective chronological order in which to supply basic goods and services. Since children must be simultaneously healthy and nourished in order to learn, the present example of helping the rural poor calls for the simultaneous supply of all three services.

Resources

The next element of the ideal compact is a commitment of resources that is sufficient to achieve the objectives. The resource commitment is perhaps the best measure of the sincerity of government in pursuing the basic needs objective. The resource commitment must be long-term and predictable.

The resource commitment should take into account the full income of potential beneficiaries. This means counting not only earned income, but also basic goods and services that are produced through home production and those supplied by other organizations such as NGOs.

It will be argued in chapters 8 and 9 that the resources for satisfying the basic needs of the poor should be paid for by a progressive tax that falls primarily on the wealthy. Taxing the poor to pay for basic goods and services is tantamount to taking with the left hand and giving with the right. It greatly slows the satisfaction of basic needs. The poor may gain a new school house, for example, but if they have to pay for it out of their own pockets, their children may be more malnourished than before, and therefore less able to learn. Progressive taxation is especially appropriate in Latin America where inequality is more extreme than anywhere else in the world.

Organizations

Establishing a compact requires identifying the organizations that are to provide the basic goods and services. The options for supplying public goods and services include public enterprises, NGOs, private enterprises that are contracted by the government, households and communities.

The criteria for selecting organizations are: (1) their ability to minimize cost, (2) the political environment, and (3) the ease of monitoring. Competitive bidding for projects can help to ensure that costs are minimized. If the political environment is one in which the government seeks reelection through serving nonpoor special interests, or if it is difficult to monitor outcomes, it may be best to encourage altruistic NGOs to supply basic goods and services to the poor.

Households and communities are generally very significant producers of basic goods and services for own-consumption. Costs can be reduced by encouraging their participation in the production of public goods and services such as roads and preventive health care. This type of participation can also help to make the poor subjects of their own development.

In order to avoid wasteful duplications of effort, supply organizations must be coordinated. It is costly for a community to spend time and effort to build a road and then have the government come in and do the same thing over again. It is better to coordinate and to build one, low-cost, high-quality road.

Incentives

Failures to reach poor people with services can usually be attributed to a misalignment between the incentives facing providers and outcomes (World Bank, 2003, p. 96). If the objective is rural education, but teaching positions are assigned on the basis of political patronage, the objective is unlikely to be reached. The incentive given to teachers is to support the politician who appointed them, not to teach well. The ideal compact must give provider organizations powerful incentives to achieve the basic needs objectives. How can this be accomplished?

Decentralized Management

Incentive creation begins with decentralizing management. The ideal is for policymakers to clearly delegate general powers and responsibilities to the management of provider organizations. Then the managers should be left free to manage frontline providers: they should be able to hire workers, to supervise them, to offer rewards for good service, and to impose sanctions for poor performance (including firing them).

Realizing the ideal of decentralized management requires that local management be competent. Achieving the required level competency may require training programs that are directed by higher levels of government.

Monitoring Organizational Outcomes

Aligning incentives with objectives requires that policymakers monitor the outcomes that provider organizations achieve. Effective monitoring begins by clearly separating the role of policymaker from that of the organizational provider. This separation frees the policymaker to focus on outcomes. If the policymaker takes on the task of providing basic services, concern with day-to-day problems tends to divert attention away from the overall, long-term impact of programs, and it undermines monitoring. The separation of roles not only gives the provider organization the incentive of knowing that its outcomes are going to be monitored, it also helps the provider to respond to the incentive by insulating it from social and political pressures to use resources for purposes other than satisfying the basic needs of the poor.

Effective monitoring requires good information not just about inputs such as the number of teachers hired, but also about outcomes such as test scores. Measuring the outcomes for health, education and other social services is not always easy. Test scores may adequately reflect certain educational goals, but abstract thinking is not so easily measured. Nevertheless, it is not impossible. Mortality rates, literacy rates, and the purity of water can be observed and measured. However, developing new and better measures of outcomes is a continuing challenge.

Policymakers can improve the monitoring of provider organizations by enlisting the help of others. Self-monitoring by the provider organizations themselves as seen in annual reports can provide useful information. Citizens/clients can be asked to generate the citizen report cards and the public expenditure tracking surveys that are described below.

Contingent Resources

Once the information about outcomes is generated, resources must be made dependent upon objective achievement. One way is the use of legally enforceable contracts that align resource distribution with organizational outcomes. Legally enforceable contracts are most suitable when outcomes are easy to monitor. A difficulty with contracts is that the policymaker is often dependent upon the information generated by the provider organization, and this information can be falsified or, less pejoratively, presented in too favorable a light. Making resources dependent upon achievement is facilitated in an environment of competition between providers: if one fails to achieve, a different provider can be hired.

Future Development

Monitoring provider organizations not only aligns incentives with outcomes, it also helps policymakers to plan future development projects and programs. Development is an ongoing process that takes place over successive time periods. In each period, the satisfaction of some basic needs creates a larger pool of resources, some of which can be invested in satisfying other basic needs in the future. Also, in each time period, some efforts succeed while others fail.

In order to maximize long-term development, policymakers need to know what does work and why, and what does *not* work and why. Armed with this information, they can reduce the waste of resources and design ever more effective compacts in future time periods. Monitoring provides feedback which makes it possible to learn from doing, and so to minimize the time required to satisfy all basic needs.

Client Power

Citizens not only voice their preferences to the state, but also to organizational providers through what is called "client power." Citizens must interact with providers because policymakers cannot specify all the actions of organizational providers in the compact. providers are necessarily left to make internal policies specific to the organization. Client power helps to assure that internal provider policies serve the needs of the poor.

Client power is a complex relationship that consists not only of expressing preferences, but also of monitoring the providers' delivery of services. Two powerful tools of monitoring are tracer studies and citizen report cards. Tracer studies "trace" government spending on a single good or service. They are most effective if political interest is high, if responsibility is clear, and if there are no complicated issues of quality measurements.

Citizen report cards are ratings by citizens of service access and quality. They include reports on corruption and general grievances about public services. An advantage of the report cards is that they look directly at public service outputs (quality and quantity) rather than inputs (budgets committed and delivered, etc.). A disadvantage is that they do not provide voters with information about decisions that specific policymakers have made. Nor do they give voters information about service benchmarks, except to the extent that the agencies themselves have established service standards. So it can be hard for voters to assess, on the basis of one report card, whether the results justify voting against the incumbent in the next election.

When does client power matter the most? It is especially important to develop and exercise client power where politicians and providers try to get reelected by spending public resources to benefit special interests. Also, client power can be very helpful in smoothing the difficulties associated with heterogeneous populations, and in improving monitoring in those cases in which it is especially difficult. The exercise of client power is less urgent if the politics are pro-poor, if the population is homogeneous, and if monitoring by the government is easy.

Client power can be developed. One way is to have the money follow the client. For example, payments by government to schools (and teachers) can depend upon the number of students enrolled. Alternatively, vouchers can be issued to citizen-consumers.

Another way to increase client power is to form coalitions that represent the interests of the poor such as parent-teach associations and health committees. The coalitions may be strengthened by including the nonpoor. Including the nonpoor is facilitated by establishing inclusive objectives such as high quality education for all children.

Decentralization can increase client power. More specifically, managerial decentralization gives greater autonomy of decision making to schools, hospitals, clinics and other providers. If managers are free to supervise staff, control pay and impose sanctions for poor performance, they have the flexibility required to adapt to clients' varying needs.

Client power can be institutionalized through a variety of mechanisms. Surveys of client preferences can be made standard policy. The law may mandate that community members be placed on planning boards and that community assemblies approve policies.

Delivery

The ideal is that services be delivered to the low-income persons who demand them and for whom they are intended. However, in fact outcomes for the delivery of basic goods and services are substantially worse for poor people than for the nonpoor, even though the poor form the majority of the populations of developing countries (World Bank, 2003, p. 20). In Peru, for example, more than 80 percent of the 15- to 19-year-olds who come from the richest fifth of the population finish the ninth grade, while only 20% of those from the poorest fifth finish (World Bank, 2003, Figure 1.2, p. 21). Why?

Services fail poor people because of a breakdown in one or more of the relationships of the service delivery model. Voice may fail because politicians have a strong incentive to cater to special interests, to core supporters, or to swing voters. The compact may fail because services are not adequately financed through progressive taxation. Client power may fail because providers are inadequately trained or because the goods and services are captured by elites. In short, a breakdown in any of the many elements of the service delivery framework may cause services to fail to reach the poor.

Reform is possible. The service delivery framework identifies the agents and the relationships that must be strong in order to achieve effective delivery of basic goods and services to the poor. Weaknesses can be improved upon in at least three ways. First, pro-poor coalitions that include both the poor and the nonpoor can increase voice and client power. Second episodes of reform often depend on reform champions such as politicians or professional associations. Linking the efforts of these "insiders" and "technocrats" to broader coalitions of citizens is often a key element of success. Third, reform is often enhanced by adopting a policy of strategic incrementalism—by beginning with an issue that is clear, politically important, and winnable.

ALL ELEMENTS

Finally, all elements of the service delivery model (voice, compact, and client power) must be sound. Service delivery can break down if any one element is missing. For example, if voice is missing, government may not supply the most needed goods and services. If compact is weak, poor planning can undermine the effectiveness of resource usage. If client power is weak, the benefits may be captured by elites.

Checklist

Box 3.1 summarizes the conclusions of this chapter by providing a checklist that can be used to design an effective decentralization process.

BOX 3.1 SERVICE DELIVERY CHECKLIST

1. Citizen Voice
   a. Do poor citizens have a strong voice in setting objectives for basic goods and services?
   b. Do poor citizens evaluate the performance of politicians?
   c. Is the information necessary to evaluate politicians easily available?
   d. Is voice captured by local elites?
   e. Are voice mechanisms institutionalized (e.g. regular community assemblies)?
2. Compact
   a. Are objectives clearly defined by policymakers and provider organizations?
   b. Are basic needs sectors chosen to meet the objectives?
   c. Are basic goods and services linked and phased?
   d. Are basic goods and services appropriately targeted to the poor?
   e. Are the resources sufficient to achieve the objective?
   f. Are the resources provided through progressive taxation?
   g. Are the most efficient and effective organizations selected to supply BN?
   h. If more than one organization supplies, are they coordinated?
   i. Are incentives aligned with objectives?
   j. Does the state monitor policymakers?
3. Client Power
   a. Is management decentralized?
   b. Do clients have a strong voice in setting the specific objectives of organizational providers?
   c. Do clients participate in the supply of basic goods and services?
   d. Do clients participate in evaluating provider outcomes?
   e. Is client power captured by local elites?
   f. Is client power institutionalized?
4. Delivery
   a. Do the program's basic goods and services reach the poor?
5. All Elements
   a. Are all elements of the model (voice, compact, and client power) sound?

CONCLUSION

The service delivery model describes an ideal process of satisfying the basic needs of the poor. The process consists of three agents (citizens, policymakers, and providers) playing key roles (voice, compact and client power). In the model, citizens, especially poor citizens, are sovereign. They guide the process of satisfying basic needs by expressing their needs and priorities to government and providers. They participate in construction, where appropriate, and in monitoring. The poor are the subjects of their own development, not mere passive "recipients" of government largess. The state and providers respond to poor citizens by supplying the basic goods and services that they require.

The result of effective service delivery is an inclusive development process. Low income citizens become more productive through being able to read, through being healthy and nourished, and through having other basic needs satisfied. Previously wasted resources are activated. The economy becomes more efficient and grows more rapidly. Citizens who were virtually excluded from the development process are empowered to produce more, to contribute more, to earn more, and to live a fuller life.

Chapter 4 introduces the role of decentralization in satisfying basic needs and establishing an inclusive development process. The chapter expands the service delivery model of this chapter in order to account for decentralization. Subsequent chapters use the expanded model to analyze the strengths and weaknesses of decentralized development programs in Latin America and to help policymakers of future programs improve on past efforts.

CHAPTER 4

DECENTRALIZATION FOR SATISFYING BASIC NEEDS

"The community has no voice; here there are no leaders."

—Indigent Person of Panama

INTRODUCTION

Decentralization is a progressive process of transferring revenue and spending decisions from the central government to subnational entities like states and municipalities (Aghón, 1993, p. 8; Blandón de Grajeda, 2003, p. 979). In short, it brings the economic functions of government (taxing and spending) closer to the people. It is a progressive process because planning and time are required to prepare lower levels of government to assume their new responsibilities.

Decentralization can help to satisfy the basic needs of the poor in many ways. Bringing government closer to the people can strengthen the voice of the voiceless. It can give government the flexibility necessary to respond to the differing needs of the poor between local jurisdictions. It can increase the participation of the poor in supplying basic goods and services. It can lower the costs of production. It can improve monitoring and create stronger incentives for government and providers to deliver basic goods and services effectively.

Decentralization for Satisfying Basic Needs: An Economic Guide for Policymakers, 2nd Edition
pp. 41–52

And yet despite its many potential advantages, if decentralization is poorly instituted, it may actually reduce the satisfaction of basic needs and worsen underdevelopment. Local elites can capture the process (and the basic goods and services that were intended for the poor). Social polarization or a lack of information may undermine the political process. Local governments may lack the capacity to tax and spend effectively. And, as we will see below, local governments are less capable than the central government of efficiently financing basic goods and services through progressive taxation.

Decentralization does not automatically satisfy the basic needs of the poor, and it is not an automatic cure-all for poverty, inequality and underdevelopment. In order to make decentralization work, it is important to identify both the potential and the obstacles within each country, and to design the decentralization process that best fits the circumstances. The purpose of this chapter is to help policymakers to meet this challenge.

The chapter is divided into two sections. The first presents a model that provides the theoretical underpinnings of decentralization. Section two describes in greater detail various forms that decentralization can take, and some of the main strengths and weaknesses of each form. The challenge for policymakers is to institute the degree of decentralization that contributes most to satisfying the basic needs of the poor, taking into account both the potential and the obstacles to decentralization in their jurisdictions.

THE MODEL

Figure 4.1 expands the service delivery framework of chapter 3 to include the process of decentralization.

Level of Government

The figure distinguishes the central government from subnational government. There are normally two levels of subnational government, the state and the municipality. We will see in chapter 6 that the state of Tlaxcala, Mexico has created a fourth level of government, the community.

Which level of subnational government is appropriate for delivering basic goods and services to the poor? The economic theory of fiscal federalism provides guidance in answering this question.

Which Level Should Supply Basic Goods and Services?

The economic theory of fiscal federalism indicates that the appropriate level of subnational government is the level whose jurisdiction encompasses the beneficiaries of a service (Oates, 1972, chapter 2). The central

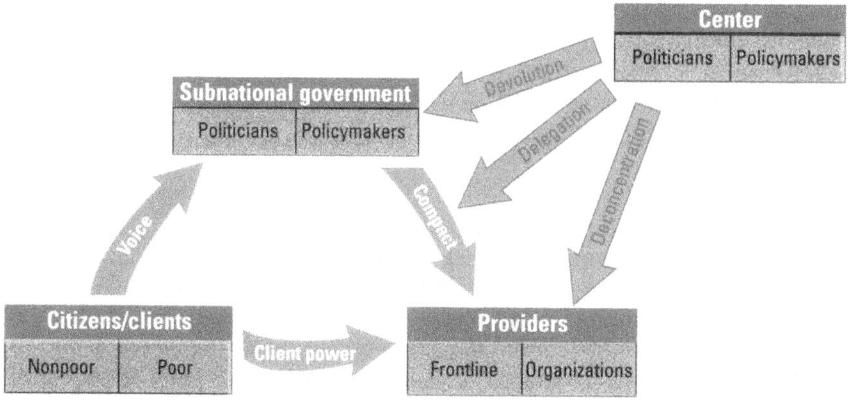

Source: World Bank (2003, p. 188).

Figure 4.1. Decentralization model.

government should supply goods and services that benefit the entire nation. Lower levels of government should supply the goods and services, the benefits of which are confined to their jurisdictions. This is called the principle of correspondence: the level of government should correspond to the area containing the beneficiaries.

This follows from the fact that the benefits of some public goods are confined to geographical subsets of the total population. The benefits of basic goods and services (primary education, basic health services, nutrition, housing, water, and sanitation) are usually confined mainly to the state and local levels.

A second crucial fact is that preferences often vary among residents of different communities. The needs of the poor in rural areas may be quite distinct from those in urban areas. The needs of the poor in large urban areas may differ from those in small ones. The needs of a locality at any point in time depend upon the history of satisfying basic needs in the locality.

Decentralization enables local governments to tailor supply to the differing preferences of subsets of society. It strengthens the voice of the people, and it gives government the flexibility to respond to that voice. Social welfare is increased by governments providing the particular goods and services that correspond more closely to the varying tastes of consumers across jurisdictions.

In contrast, it is difficult for one central government that is supplying basic goods and services to know the differences in preferences, much less cater to those differences. Centralization tends to lead to everybody receiving more or less the same thing. Variations in preferences are largely ignored. People are forced to consume more goods and services that are not their top priority. Social welfare is diminished.

The theory of fiscal federalism concludes with the decentralization theorem:

> For a public good—the consumption of which is defined over geographical subsets of the total population, and for which the costs of providing each level of output of the good in each jurisdiction are the same for the central or the respective local government—it will always be more efficient (or at least as efficient) for local governments to provide the efficient levels of output for their respective jurisdictions than for the central government to provide *any* specified and uniform level of output across all jurisdictions (Oates, 1972, p. 35).

Which Level Should Redistribute Income?

Efficient financing of the basic needs for the poor requires a redistribution of income that consists largely of taxing the wealthy in order to pay for supplying basic goods and services to the poor. The theory of fiscal federalism argues that it is difficult for the local government to accomplish this redistribution (Oates, 1972, pp. 6-8, 31-33).

The formal argument is that if a municipality adopts a *significantly more aggressive* policy of redistributing income than surrounding local governments, it creates an incentive for the wealthy to move out to neighboring municipalities, and for the poor to migrate into the community. If this were to occur, a more nearly equal distribution of income might result, but it would be caused largely by an outflow of the rich and an influx of the poor with a fall in the level of per-capita income in the community (Oates, 1972, p. 7). The mobility of both rich and poor residents would undermine the municipality's relatively aggressive redistribution effort.

The standard conclusion is that municipalities should avoid engaging in redistributive policies. Since mobility across national boundaries is generally much more difficult than that within a nation, a policy of income redistribution should be carried out primarily on the national level (Oates, 1972, p. 8). Redistributing income is generally a function of the center.

We might add that municipalities are sometimes segregated by income class. There are rich municipalities and there are poor municipalities. The rich municipalities have very little need to redistribute income in order to satisfy basic needs. The poor municipalities have very little capacity to redistribute income. Hence, decentralization in the context of municipalities that are segregated by income class reduces the redistribution of income that is necessary for satisfying the basic needs of the poor.

The limited capacity of municipalities to redistribute income calls into question the very notion of decentralizing taxing powers in order to satisfy the basic needs of the poor. Insofar as municipalities have only limited powers to redistribute income, transferring taxing powers from the central to local governments reduces the nation's capacity to redistribute income, and it thereby slows the satisfaction of basic needs that is necessary for inclusive development. Leading economist Richard Musgrave concludes that "Decentralization reduces the capacity to undertake redistributional policies. Implications for such policies are therefore a strategic factor in the centralization-versus-decentralization issue" (Musgrave & Musgrave, 1989, p. 459).

Do Municipalities Have Any Redistributive Role?

The preceding argument shows that there are limits to the amount of income redistribution that municipalities can undertake, but the argument assumes an extreme case that departs from reality in some important ways. More realistic assumptions suggest that some room for redistribution on the local level may remain.

The first assumption of the standard argument is that a municipality engages in "significantly more aggressive" redistributive policies than surrounding jurisdictions. This implies that a local government can engage in more or less the same degree of redistribution that surrounding localities conduct without danger of migration undermining the program. If all municipalities are engaging in approximately the same level of redistribution, no resident would gain from moving to another jurisdiction in order to avoid it.

Second, the precise meaning of "significantly more aggressive" is not clear. How much extra redistribution can a municipality undertake without causing migration that undermines the process? A number of factors could diminish migration in response to relatively aggressive redistribution policies. They include friendships with other members of the community, a willingness to help the poor within one's own jurisdiction, the cost in time and money of moving, access to work or shopping, cultural amenities, and the quality of the school system and other public services such as police protection. Zoning, the high cost of housing, high taxes, and cultural differences could prevent the poor from moving in.

The knowledge of the "extra" redistribution programs in any one municipality may be quite imperfect. People may not know the amount of redistribution that takes place in their own municipality, much less that of others. It would seem that only in a very extreme case would a municipality gain the reputation for "soaking the rich" that would be necessary to drive the rich away and attract unmanageable numbers of the poor.

Mobility decreases with the size of the jurisdiction and with the failure to provide a rapid and inexpensive mode of transportation. Mexico City, for example, is a very large municipality with a severely inadequate transportation network. Migration to avoid redistribution is surely restricted by the fact that acute traffic congestion makes it very costly to commute long distances. A wealthy person living in a small town, on the other hand, might be more easily driven out by an aggressive redistribution program.

The conclusion is that mobility places limits on the capacity of government to undertake redistribution for satisfying the basic needs of the poor, and that mobility varies with the size of the jurisdiction. States are more capable of redistributing income than Municipalities, and central governments are more capable than states. However, this does not mean that subcentral governments should abandon all efforts to redistribute income in order to satisfy basic needs. However, the capacity for effective redistribution is greatest at the central government level, and as a result it would make sense for the central government to assume primary responsibility for redistributing income.

Agents and Roles

Figure 4.1 shows that the same three agents (citizens, politicians and providers) and the same three relationships (voice, compact and client power) determine the quality of service delivery on the subnational level. All that was said in chapter 3 about the relationships between the agents of service delivery applies to the subnational level. The role of decentralization is to strengthen the agents and their relationships.

Degrees of Decentralization

The three arrows of Figure 4.1 leading from the center to the subnational government indicate that three degrees of decentralization are possible: "deconcentration," "delegation," and "devolution." Deconcentration is the lowest degree of decentralization; it consists mainly of the territorial redistribution of central government offices and personnel (Blandón, 2003, p. 979). The highest degree of decentralization is devolution. Here, both taxing and spending powers are decentralized to subnational governments. Delegation is an intermediate form of decentralization.

Table 4.1 distinguishes each degree of decentralization by its political, fiscal and administration features. The political feature addresses the strength of voice that local citizens have in demanding basic goods and services. The fiscal feature addresses the tasks of raising and spending revenues. The administrative feature addresses the supply of basic goods and services by providers.

Deconcentration

Political deconcentration exists if local government is appointed by and accountable to the center. Its strength is that it can counter the capture of local government by elites. Its weakness is that citizen voice is remote and relatively weak.

Fiscal deconcentration exists if all funds and spending decisions come from the center. The greatest strength of fiscal deconcentration is that it facilitates the redistribution that is necessary for satisfying the basic needs of the poor in the shortest possible time. This implies that the tax system of the central government be progressive.

The weakness of fiscal deconcentration is that the heterogeneity of needs across jurisdictions is not taken into account. Also, central control of the supply of goods and services can be a source of central government using its power to manipulate the electorate, although the danger of this can be reduced by rule-based allocations and by monitoring. Expenditures are not closely tied to local taxes, and so people tend to over-consume public goods and services. However, this weakness loses significance in our case of supplying subsidized basic goods and services to the poor.

Administrative deconcentration exists if the provider staff working at the local level are employees of the center and accountable to the center; the center merely relocates its offices to local jurisdictions. The greatest strength of administrative deconcentration is that it compensates for weak administrative capacity at the local level. Also, administrative deconcentration can be used to train subnational staff. Its weakness is that client power and accountability to local citizens can be weak; this can be overcome to some extent by a strong compact.

Devolution

Political devolution exists if local politicians are elected by, and accountable to, the local electorate. The strength of political devolution is that voice can be very strong. The weakness is that local government can be captured by local elites. Also, social polarization and uninformed voting can divert the political process away from satisfying basic needs.

Fiscal devolution exists if local government controls the spending decisions; funding comes mainly from the local jurisdiction, although it may be supplemented by the center. The strength of fiscal devolution is that each local government is free to supply the goods and services that address the unique needs of its population. The fiscal process is efficient in so far as spending is limited by the willingness of local citizens to pay.

Table 4.1. Degrees of Decentralization

Degree of Decentralization	*Political Features (Demand)*	*Fiscal Features (Revenue/Spending)*	*Administrative Features (Supply)*
Deconcentration	• No elected local government • Local government appointed by, and accountable to, the central government. • Weak local voice	• All funds from center • Local government is delivery arm of center • No local discretion over services	• Staff are employees of, and accountable to, center • Weak local capacity • Weak client power
Devolution	• Local government is locally elected and accountable to local electorate • Strong local voice	• Subject to nationally set minimum standards, local government can allocate resources • Funds mainly from local revenues.	• Staff are employees of local government • Local government has full discretion over salary levels, staffing numbers, and allocation, and authority to hire and fire • Labor standards and procedures may be established in civil service framework • Strong client power
Delegation	• Local government elected locally, but it is partially accountable to center. • More local Voice, but it can be overruled by center	• Most funds from center. • Spending priorities and norms from center • Some local authority over allocation of resources to meet local circumstances	• Staff could be employees of central or local government, but pay and employment conditions set by center • Local government may have some authority over hiring and management of staff, but less able to fire.

Source: World Bank (2003, Table 10.2, p. 189).

The weakness of fiscal devolution is that it minimizes the possibility of redistributing income for satisfying the basic needs of the poor. Fiscal devolution accentuates regional disparities. A very poor jurisdiction has very limited ability to tax, and so the basic needs of its people remain unfulfilled. A rich region is easily able to tax, and so both the basic and nonbasic needs of its citizens are satisfied with the result that it continues to grow and develop.

Administrative devolution exists if providers are employees of the local government and fully responsible to it. The strength of administrative devolution is that client power tends to be strongest. The weakness is that local administrative capacity may be weak. Also, strong client power can have its negative side—local administration may be distracted away from satisfying the basic needs of the poor by social polarization and uninformed citizens.

Delegation

Political delegation is an intermediate position between deconcentration and devolution. Here, local government is elected and to some extent controlled by local citizens, but it is still partially accountable to the center. The strength of political delegation is that local citizens have more voice than in the case of deconcentration. Whether the center's control over local government is a strength or weakness depends upon the quality of local and central politics. If, for example, local government is controlled by local elites who have no interest in satisfying the basic needs of the poor, and if the central government has a pro poor orientation, then the center's control over local government contributes to the satisfaction of basic needs.

Fiscal delegation exists if spending priorities and program standards are set centrally, but local government has some authority to adjust the allocation of resources to meet local circumstances; all funding is provided by the central government.

The strength of fiscal delegation is that the central government may have an expertise to design program standards that is lacking to local governments. It may also limit capture of the decentralization process by local elites. At the same time, local government is left some flexibility to adjust to local circumstances. Central funding makes it possible to redistribute income and achieve a time-efficient satisfaction of the basic needs of the poor.

The weakness of fiscal delegation can be that the flexibility of the local government is limited. This is a drawback in cases in which the local government is competent and in which the needs of the local poor are quite distinct. Another weakness is that local government is left little discretion to tax and spend. Even if the district is very poor, more discretion to do so might improve social welfare.

Administrative delegation exists if local government has the ability to hire and, within limits, manage the staff, but pay, employment conditions and firing are determined centrally. The strength of administrative delegation is that it gives more client power to local citizens than administrative deconcentration. The great weakness of administrative delegation is that setting pay and firing are two key instruments of control over employees. Centralizing these powers greatly reduces the ability of local government to respond to clients and to manage its staff effectively.

Many Combinations Are Possible

Many combinations of decentralization are possible. A country, for example, might adopt a combination of political devolution in which local government is accountable to the local electorate and fiscal deconcentration in which all funds come from the center. In practice, decentralization often involves a mix of deconcentration, delegation and devolution.

Once again, the appropriate mix depends upon the circumstances in which the government is operating. Careful planning and execution are required. The degree of decentralization may apply to a government, or to a program for supplying basic goods and services.

Summary

Table 4.2 provides a summary of important strengths and weaknesses of each type of decentralization. It can be used with Box 3.1 to evaluate decentralization programs. The reader is encouraged to identify other strengths and weaknesses. The challenge to policymakers is identify and institute the form of decentralization that best accommodates country circumstances. Programs can be evaluated by first identifying the degree of decentralization and then asking whether it suits the political, fiscal and administrative circumstances.

CONCLUSION

In the ideal world, there is no need for a redistribution of income, no ignorance, no capture of voice and client power by elites, and no lack of administrative skills. Under these circumstances, the ideal degree of decentralization is "devolution." Devolution gives voice and client power to the "voiceless" poor. The most appropriate level of government responds to the particular needs of its jurisdiction. Compacts between governments and providers include guidelines for supplying basic goods and services. Beneficiaries are taxed to pay for the goods and services that they receive, thus assuring efficient quantities of output. Providers use the guidelines of the compact, the voice of clients, and their skills to deliver efficiently and effectively the basic goods and services needed. Under these circumstances, devolution does the best job of satisfying basic needs and generating an inclusive development process.

Table 4.2. Strengths and Weaknesses of Decentralization

Degree of Decentralization	*Strengths*	*Weaknesses*
Deconcentration		
Political	Minimize capture by local elites	Weak voice of the poor
Fiscal	Facilitate redistribution of income	Insensitive to diversity of preferences
Administrative	Compensate for lack of subnational capacity	Weak client power
Devolution		
Political	Maximize voice of the poor	Capture by local elites; social polarization and uninformed voting may undermine political process
Fiscal	Cater to diversity of preferences; efficient supply	Minimize capacity for redistribution of income.
Administrative	Maximize client power	Lack of local capacity
Delegation		
Political	Balance voice with control of local elites	Reduced voice; central elites may undermine control
Fiscal	Balance local discretion with central priorities and standards; Accommodate redistribution	Limited flexibility to respond to heterogeneity
Administrative	Balance compensation for a lack of subnational capacity with some client power	Lack of control over staff

In the real world, extreme poverty and inequality generate a need for a redistribution of income, partly because they silence the poor and empower elites to capture governments. A lack of education generates ignorance. Culture, history, ignorance and greed contribute to social polarization. Governments lack administrative skills. These realities can undermine the positive effects of devolution. Until they are overcome, different mixes of decentralization may be preferable.

The models of this chapter indicate that there are three degrees of decentralization and three features of each degree. Multiple combinations of degrees and features are possible, each having its own advantages and disadvantages. The first challenge facing each government is to assess the political, fiscal and administrative circumstances in which it operates, and to design the decentralization program that best takes advantage of those circumstances. The second challenge is to advance the process of decentralization over time.

In future chapters, we will assess various decentralization programs in light of the models presented in chapters 3 and 4. We will examine how each program responded to the circumstances in which it operates. We will see creativity in the design of the programs, and we will see that each program has both strengths and weaknesses. The goal is to learn from these examples to design decentralization programs that are ever more effective in satisfying the basic needs of the poor.

PART III

CASE STUDIES

CHAPTER 5

TRANSFER-LED DECENTRALIZATION IN MEXICO

"Decentralized levels of government need not levy their own taxes"

—Wallace E. Oates

INTRODUCTION

More than 12 million Mexicans live on less than $2 a day. Countless more are living in dire need. The richest 10% of Mexicans receives 25 times the income of the poorest 10%. The country's infant mortality rate is almost 4 times higher than that of the United States (Tables 1.2, 1.3, and 1.5).

How does Mexico's process of decentralization respond to these circumstances? Is it effective in giving low income Mexicans an opportunity to overcome their poverty by incorporating them into the development process? The purpose of this chapter is to address these questions.

The chapter begins with an overview of the country's grant system, and a description of the one grant that is specifically oriented toward meeting the basic needs of the poor, the *FAIS* (*Fondo de Aportaciones para la Infraestructura Social*; Social Infrastructure Fund). Next, the system is evaluated

Decentralization for Satisfying Basic Needs: An Economic Guide for Policymakers, 2nd Edition
pp. 53–67

in the light of the decentralization theory of chapters 3-4. The chapter concludes with recommendations for policymakers.

OVERVIEW

Centralization

Mexico's process of decentralization is rooted in history. At the beginning of the twentieth century, the country was in financial disarray. The tax authority was weak. Public expenditure was financed by debt and printing money. Each level of government had its own revenue system. Different levels of government taxed the same item. A multiplicity of rates, fines and penalties made the financial system complex and inefficient (Giugale & Webb, 2000, pp. 123-124).

As a remedy, the federal government began a process of fiscal *centralization* in which almost all taxes came to be collected by the central government. Local governments agreed to limit their taxing in return for revenue transfers from the federal government. States and municipalities were not forced to give up their taxing authority, but the ability to receive not only tax revenues, but also revenues from the oil industry, as well as avoiding the political costs of imposing taxes, made voluntary participation in the system an attractive choice (Giugale & Webb, 2000, pp. 126-127). Mexico's financial system became highly centralized.

Transfer-Led Decentralization

Mexico has begun to reverse its process of fiscal centralization by instituting a remarkable amount of financial grants from the central government to states and municipalities. In 1999, the federal government transferred no less than 39% of its total budget to state and local governments. Transfers are now the largest single item in the federal budget. The 1999 transfers were larger than the 30% of the budget dedicated to pay for all the expenditures of the central ministries (Giugale & Webb, 2000, p. 206).

The importance of transfers for Mexican states is indicated by the fact that in 1999, taxes represented only about 4.5% of the total revenues (Giugale & Webb, 2000, p. 16).[1]

Municipal governments are on average only slightly less dependent than the states on transfers from the central government.

There are varying estimates of the portion of municipal budgets that come from transfers, but all agree that the portion is high. Giugale and

Webb estimated that in 1999 municipal governments received about two-thirds of their total net revenues from transfers (Giugale & Webb, 2000, p. 16). Courchene and Díaz-Cayeros, estimated that in the same year the municipalities received 80% of their revenues from intergovernmental transfers (Giugale & Webb, 2000, p. 220). Mexico's Secretaría de Hacienda y Crédito Público reported that in 1999 Mexican municipalities received no less than 91.7% of their revenues in the form of transfers (Raich, 2005, p. 11). In contrast, Chilean municipalities received only 5.7% of their revenues from transfers in 1999. The average for all of Latin America was 39.4%, less than half of Mexico's percentage.

MEXICO'S GRANT SYSTEM

Table 5.1 lists selected features of Mexico's extensive grant system as it existed in 1999. Column (2) of the table, *Ramo* ("Item"), shows that there are two main categories of transfers in Mexico: *Participaciones* (Ramo 28) and *Aportaciones* (Ramo 33).

Participaciones

Participaciones were originally revenues of states and municipalities whose collection was delegated to the federal level in order to correct the chaotic tax situation that existed among lower levels of government. The federal government is legally bound to collect the taxes and to return the money to the areas from which it came. Column (4), "Type of Expenditure," indicates that *participaciones* are generally used to pay current operating expenses. Any effect on satisfying basic needs is indirect.

In principle, the federal government merely acts as a collection agent for the state and local governments. However, in practice, there is some movement toward using *participaciones* to redistribute income from relatively wealthy to relatively poor regions. Column (5), "Nature of Allocation," indicates that the allocation of *participaciones* is either "equal," or by "derivation." "Equal" means that the funds are distributed on an equal per capita basis. "Derivation" means in effect that the funds are returned to the area from which they are derived.[2] The largest *participación* fund, the *Fondo General de Participaciones (FGP)*, is being shifted from a derivation to an equal per capita basis. This is causing the participaciones to be distributed fairly equally across states (Giugale & Webb, 2000, p. 208).

Column (6) of Table 5.1 indicates that the *participaciones* are transferred unconditionally. This means that the federal government does not impose conditions on the ways in which the grants are spent. However,

Table 5.1. Federal Funds Transferred to States and Municipalities, 1999 (Millions of Pesos)

(1)	*(2)*	*(3)*	*(4)*	*(5)*	*(6)*	*(7)*
Fund	*Ramo*	*Amount*	*Type of Expenditure*	*Type of Transfer*	*Nature of Allocation*	*Formula*
General de Participaciones (FGP)	28	117,801	States must transfer at least 20% to municipalities	Unconditional	Equal	Yes
De Fomento Municipal (FFM)	28	5,559	Mostly current	Unconditional	Derivation	Yes
Tenencia	28	7,984	Works as own revenue in practice	Unconditional	Derivation	100%
Automóviles nuevos (ISAN)	28	3,255	Works as own revenue in practice	Unconditional	Derivation	100%
Impuestos especiales	28	2,600	Mostly current	Unconditional	Derivation	Yes
Other revenue sharing	28	1,437	Mostly current	Unconditional	Derivation	No
de Aportaciones para la Educación Básica y Normal (FAEB)	33	86,481	Current (teacher payrolls in basic education)	Condicional	Equal	No**
de Aportaciones para Servicios de Salud (FASS)	33	14,466	Current (doctors and nurses payrolls)	Condicional	Equal	No***
de Aportaciones para la Infraestructura Social Municipal (FAISM)	33	12,245	Capital investment in the municipalities (Public Works)	Condicional	Compensatory	Yes
de Aportaciones para la Infraestructura Social Estatal (FAISE)	33	1,689	Capital investment, States can assign according to own criteria to municipalities	Condicional	Compensatory	Yes

de Aportaciones para el Fortalecimiento de los municipios (FAFM)	33	13,098	Current, although recommended to spend on specific items: public debt and safety	Unconditional	Equal	Yes
de Aportaciones Multiples (FAM)	33	4,537	Current and capital (school breakfasts and school construction)	Conditional	Equal	No**
de Aportaciones para la Educación Tecnológica de Adultos (FAEA)	33/11	1,251	Current (technical institutes)	Conditional	Equal	No**
de Aportaciones para la Seguridad Pública de los Estados y del Distrito Federal (FASP)	33	4.700	Current, though some capital equipment	Condicional	Derivation	Yes
de Aportaciones para los servicios de educación básica en el Distrito Federal	25	10,767	Current (teacher payroll)	Condicional	n.a.	No
Previsiones salariales por FAEB	25	10,935	Current (teacher pay raises)	Conditional	Equal	No**
Previsiones salariales por FASSA	12	1,696	Current (doctor and nurse raises)	Conditional	Equal	No**
Previsiones salariales	23	1,966	Current	Conditional	n.a.	No
Desastres Naturales	23	4,000	Current	Conditional	n.a.	No

Notes: n.a. = not applicable. **The Ley de Coordinación Fiscal does provide some vague guidelines, but they are so general that they do not become a binding formula. ***A formula exists, but only for a compensating part of the fund, which constitutes 1% of it.
Source: Giugale and Webb (2000, Table 5.1, pp. 209-210).

the grants are in fact less unconditional than may at first appear. The reality is that states and municipalities had spending commitments such as the salaries of teachers, doctors and nurses before the collection of the taxes was delegated to the federal government, and those spending commitments remain. Furthermore, wages and salaries are often set by the federal government. In the words of one state official, "our autonomy is zero" (Fuentes, 2003; Giugale & Webb, 2000, p. 52).

Aportaciones

The second main category of funds in Table 5.1 is Ramo 33, called *Aportaciones*. Column (5), "Type of transfer," indicates that the *aportaciones* are generally *conditional* grants. The grants were originally earmarked to pay for federal spending commitments that have been transferred to the states and municipalities (Giugale and Webb, 2000, p. 211).

Spending Responsibilities

The spending responsibilities of state and municipal governments have been unilaterally assigned by the central government. States have been assigned a wide variety of expenditures. Most important for satisfying basic needs, they have been assigned expenditure responsibilities in education, health, water and sewerage, roads, public security, and social assistance (Giugale & Webb, 2000, Table 3.1, pp. 140-142).

Municipalities have been assigned few spending and service delivery responsibilities, especially in education and health, where significant benefits could be realized through decentralization to the lowest decision-making unit (Giugale & Webb, 2000, p. 139). International experience shows that the delivery of educational services becomes more efficient when decentralization reaches the local level and, even more significantly, when it reaches the school level (Gershberg & Winkler, 2000; cited in Giugale & Webb, 2000, p. 156).

In education, municipal expenditures are confined to school maintenance, some school construction, and basic equipment. Municipal expenditures on education were a very modest 0.01 to 0.03% of GDP between 1992 and 1999, while consolidated government expenditures on education ranged between 4.41 and 5.21% of GDP. In the health sector, municipalities have only been assigned responsibility for basic infrastructure in the *FAIS* grant considered below (Giugale & Webb, 2000, Table 3.1, pp. 140-142).

The assignment of limited spending responsibilities to municipalities helps to compensate for their lack of administrative capacity. An official survey of municipalities in 1995 found that, depending upon the particular criterion, only 20 to 40% of Mexico's 2,400 municipalities measured up to standard measures of administrative capacity (SEGOB, CEDEMUN, y INEGI, 1995, cited in Giugale & Webb, 2000, p. 169). The weaknesses included:

- Even though the great majority of municipalities had a treasurer, only 39% had a specialized agency responsible for supervising and planning the budget process.
- About 60% of the country's municipalities did not have a computer system in 1995; accounting was done by hand in most municipalities.
- About 63% of municipalities did not have basic regulations or manuals for administrative procedures.
- In roughly 80% of the municipalities there was no statutory framework for expenditure planning. In these municipalities, the budget document was improvised and very elemental.
- In more than 70% of the municipalities there were neither basic rules nor manuals for the collection and actualization of the property tax. In fact, the state administered the property tax for the vast majority of these municipalities.
- Citizens participated in government programs in just 51% of the municipalities, almost always in public works.

FAIS

FAIS is the one federal grant that explicitly aims to satisfy the basic needs of the poor, and so this grant is a crucial determinant of the extent to which Mexico's decentralization program contributes to generating an inclusive development process. This section highlights the main attributes of the grant. The next section evaluates both *FAIS* and the grant system as a whole in light of the model of chapters 3-4.

Beneficiaries

Federal law stipulates that *FAIS* money must be spent on "projects, basic social actions and investments that directly benefit the sectors of the population that are socially marginalized and in extreme poverty" (LCF, 2009, Article 33, p. 27).

Two FAIS Grants

Column (1) of Table 5.1 shows that the *FAIS* grant is subdivided into two parts, one for the state (*FAISE*, *Fondo de Aportaciones para la Infraestructura Social Estatal*), and one for municipalities (*FAISM*, *Fondo de Aportaciones para la Infraestructura Social Municipal*).

States and municipalities are generally subject to the same laws that guide the use of the *FAIS* grant. The main difference between the two funds is that, in accord with the correspondence principle of Chapter 4, *FAISM* funds are used for projects, the benefits of which are confined to individual municipalities, while *FAISE* funds are used for projects that benefit a wider, regional population.

Resource Commitment

Article 32 of the Ley de Coordinación Fiscal states that the amount of the transfer shall equal 2.5% of the Participating Federal Revenues (LCF, 2009, p. 27). Participating Federal Revenues are tax revenues, plus fees received by the federal government from oil and mining, minus various sources of revenue (Cámara de Diputados, 2005, p. 4). Eighty-eight percent of the *FAIS* funds are designated for municipalities, while the other 12% are assigned to the states.

Column (3) of Table 5.1, "Amount," indicates that in 1999, municipalities received 12,245 million pesos, and the states were granted 1,689 million pesos. The total of 13,934 million pesos amounted to 4.5% of all grants for the year, and to 0.30% of the country's Gross Domestic Product for 1999.

Earmarking

Federal law states that the municipal funds (*FAISM*) must be used exclusively to provide the following basic infrastructure: "drinking water, sewerage, drainage and latrines, municipal urbanization (roads, street lights, etc.), electricity for rural areas and low income neighborhoods, basic health infrastructure, basic education infrastructure, housing improvements, rural roads, and rural productive infrastructure" (LCF, 2009, Article 33, p. 27). The states are left free to determine the regional projects that best serve the poor.

Formulas

Funds are distributed to the states and municipalities using one of two formulas. The first takes into account per capita income, level of education, size of house, and the availability of drainage, electricity and cooking fuel (LCF, 2009, Article 34, p. 28). If a lack of data makes it impossible to apply the first formula, then a simpler one can be used that takes into account the employed population that earns less than double the minimum wage, the illiteracy rate, access to sewerage, and access to electricity (LCF, 2009, Article 35, p. 30).

Redistribution

Column (6) of the table, "Nature of allocation," indicates that the two *FAIS* funds are the only funds that are "compensatory," meaning that the size of the grants "compensates" for the level of poverty. Since the grants are inversely related to poverty, they tend to redistribute income from the non-poor to the poor.

Participation

Article 33 of the LCF stipulates that "states and municipalities should promote the participation of the benefiting communities in determining the destination of the funds, as well as oversight, programming, construction, control, follow-up, and evaluation of the projects." In short, subnational governments are required to promote the full participation of citizens in every phase of supplying basic infrastructure.

The same article 33 of the LCF facilitates the participation of citizens in monitoring by stipulating that states and municipalities inform their inhabitants of the amounts of money that they receive, of the projects funded by those monies, the cost of each project, and its location, objective, beneficiaries and outcome. The same information must also be provided to the states and through them to the national Secretaría de Desarrollo Social (SEDESOL).

Planning

The process of supplying basic infrastructure begins with municipal governments that, together with their citizens, identify and prioritize their needs and draw up plans to satisfy them. An interview with the mayor of Naucalpan indicated that projects in her municipality are determined in two-stage process. First, community meetings are held in order to identify and prioritize needs. Second, the municipality's planning department conducts analyses in order to maximize the impact of projects: "If one street has one family living on it, and another has twenty families, we will pave the latter street first" (A. Marín, personal communication, October 17, 2003).

Municipal plans are coordinated with state and national plans by the state planning agency, COPLADE. The formal responsibilities of COPLADE include formulating and updating the state's development plan, coordinating the federal, state, and local plans, and executing and evaluating state development plans (Giugale and Webb, 2000, p. 167). State congresses must approve the budgets for all the municipalities and for the state governments.

Degree of Decentralization

The distinctive character of Mexico's decentralization is found in its assignment of responsibilities for three elements of supplying public goods and services: (1) regulation or normative design, (2) financing, and (3) implementation. In Mexico, the central government dominates the first two elements, while states, and, to a lesser extent, municipalities dominate the third element.

Consequently, Mexico's approach to decentralization is perhaps best categorized as "Delegation." It is political delegation because state and municipal governments are elected locally, but they are partially accountable to the center that establishes norms for the supply of public goods and services. It is fiscal delegation because most state and local funds come from the center, but subnational governments have some authority over the allocation of those resources. It is administrative delegation because national and subnational governments share planning and expenditures as well as control of the staff that implements the funded programs.

EVALUATION

The purpose of this section is to evaluate the capacity of Mexico's decentralization program to satisfy the basic needs of the poor within a short period of time. The models of Chapters 3 and 4 are used to identify the program's main strengths and weaknesses. This will help to determine the circumstances under which Mexico's style of decentralization is appropriate and worthy of imitation by policymakers.

Capacity for Redistribution

Certainly one of the greatest strengths of Mexico's decentralization process is that it makes possible the redistribution of income that is necessary for satisfying the basic needs of the poor within a short period of time. This is especially important in a context of extreme inequality. We saw in chapter 3 that central governments are best able to redistribute income because it is relatively difficult for citizens to undermine centralized redistribution through migration.

Central governments can redistribute income through both progressive taxation and progressive expenditures, that is, through taxes that fall relatively heavily on the nonpoor and through expenditures that benefit mainly the poor. Since Mexico's central government collects most of the taxes and sets the guidelines for many expenditures, it is in an excellent position to redistribute income. This is very important for a country characterized by extreme poverty and inequality.

Whether the central government takes advantage of this capacity depends upon whether the tax and expenditure programs are actually progressive. Preliminary indications are that Mexico's tax system is not progressive. In 1995, the central government received 26.6% of its revenues from progressive "direct" taxes such as the income tax, but it received 33.9% of its revenue from regressive "indirect" taxes such as the value added tax (Inter-American Development Bank, 1996a, Tables C-8 and C-9, pp. 373-374). Since most tax revenue came from regressive taxes, it appears that the tax system as a whole was—and is (barring radical changes since 1995)—regressive.

A recent study of expenditure incidence found that Mexico's expenditures on health and education are mildly progressive in that they lowered the Gini coefficient from approximately 0.54 to approximately 0.48 (Scott, 2001, Graph 6.1, p. 34). However, compared to seven other Latin American countries in the study, both Mexico's redistributive effort through expenditures, and its efficiency in targeting expenditures to the poor, are categorized as "Low" (Scott, 2001, Table 6.4, p. 38).

It therefore appears that Mexico's central government is not actively exploiting its opportunity to redistribute income in order to satisfy basic needs in a short time. Still, the structure of Mexico's decentralization program provides a great opportunity for the redistribution of income. Taking advantage of the opportunity will be a continuing challenge for policymakers.

Planning

The objectives of *FAIS* are clear and suitable for satisfying the infrastructure needs of the very poor. However, the grant system as a whole does not reflect a comprehensive, coherent plan to satisfy all the basic needs of the poor within a short period of time. A problem is that the system does not link the basic infrastructure provided by *FAIS* with other basic goods and services such as nutrition, health and education services

This failure to link infrastructure with other basic goods and services can undermine the effectiveness of a basic needs program fast. If, for example, the water supply is not improved, health clinics can find people returning over and over again because shortly after receiving treatment they drink impure water. The two services should be linked and supplied as a package. Linking and phasing basic goods and services require a comprehensive, coherent plan for satisfying basic needs.

Various grants help to satisfy the noninfrastructure needs of the poor, but always to some unknown extent and in an uncoordinated way. For example, the FAEB grant in support of teacher payrolls in basic education helps to educate the poor to some extent, as does the FASS grant to pay the salaries of doctors and nurses. But these grants serve both the poor and the nonpoor. To what extent do they help the poor? Are they linked to, and phased with, other basic goods and services?

The way in which the size of the *FAIS* grant is determined seems to betray a lack of planning and commitment to satisfy the basic needs of the poor within a short time. The size of *FAIS* is 2.5% of Participating Federal Revenues, not the amount of money estimated to be necessary to meet the objective of eliminating poverty. Instead of developing a comprehensive, coherent plan and implementing it, the government seems to be saying: "Infrastructure is a serious problem. Let's spend some money on it."

Various grants help to satisfy the non-infrastructure needs of the poor, but always to some unknown extent and in an uncoordinated way. For example, the FAEB grant in support to teach payrolls in basic education helps to educate the poor to some extent, as does the FASS grant to pay the salaries of doctors and nurses. But these grants serve both the poor and the non-poor. To what extent do they help the poor? Are they linked to, and phased with, other basic goods and services?

Still another indication of a lack of planning is that the grant system assigns concurrent responsibilities for basic goods and services without clearly defining the specific responsibilities. For example, in the case of education, both state and municipal governments assume vaguely defined responsibilities for the maintenance of schools. This often results in no one taking adequate responsibility for maintenance (Giugale and Webb, 2000, pp. 12, 15). The states say that a particular need is the municipality's responsibility, and the municipalities say that it is the state's responsibility. A survey conducted in 1995 found that primary schools in 55% of the country's municipalities were in urgent need of repair and maintenance, as were junior high schools in 41% of municipalities (SEGOB, CEDEMUN, and INEGI 1995; cited in Giugale and Webb, 2000, p. 148)

Instead of implementing a coherent plan to satisfy basic needs, the system appears to be more a hodgepodge of grants that were instituted in a piecemeal fashion over time. *Participaciones* were instituted to pay for specific functions that the states were already carrying out but were unable to finance properly. *Aportaciones* were originally granted to pay for goods and services, the administration of which had been decentralized. Instead of implementing a comprehensive plan, the grants reflect isolated, disconnected decisions to pay for this or that service.

The president of a Mexico City newspaper, *Zona Norte*, commented that the problem with social expenditures in Mexico is that they do not reflect a plan to achieve a specific goal. The amount of social spending is determined more by "what is left over after everything else is paid for," than by the requirements of a plan to satisfy basic needs in a short period of time. "That is why the poverty problem remains unresolved in Mexico" (López Barroso, 2004).

Separation of Taxing from Spending

The Mexican system of decentralization is propitious for redistributing income. A necessary consequence of this is that taxes are not clearly and closely related to spending. As a result, spending is not limited by citizen incomes and their willingness to pay taxes. Goods and services appear to be free, and so citizens tend to consume all that they can get. This can lead to over-consumption in the sense that the costs of providing goods and services exceed the benefits.

What is needed is a balancing act. The inefficiency of over-consumption must be weighed against the efficiency of incorporating the poor more fully and more rapidly into the production process. At present, funding for the basic needs programs is so low, and the advantages of utilizing wasted human resources are so great, that it would seem that the balance would tip in favor of the Mexican approach of centralized taxation.

FAIS

FAIS is so well structured that it has the potential for satisfying the basic needs of the poor in a short period of time. Its "compact" clearly defines the objective of providing basic infrastructure to the poor, and it clearly defines what that infrastructure is (water, etc). It promotes "voice" and "client power" by requiring subnational governments to promote the full participation of the citizens in all phases of supplying basic infrastructure from planning to monitoring. The compact employs allocation formulas that target the poor, reduce corruption and capture by elites, and it provides information that facilitates monitoring. The development plans of municipalities are coordinated with those of state and national governments. The grant redistributes income from the nonpoor to the poor, and it decentralizes administration, making it more possible to serve the distinctive needs of each jurisdiction.

Despite its many strengths, the grant is not without its weaknesses. In addition to the lack of planning described above, the grant appears to be seriously underfunded. One indication is that the grant aims to help only the "socially marginalized and extremely poor." This limit on the fund's beneficiaries seems to exclude many people who are in great need of basic infrastructure.

As mentioned earlier, more than 12 million Mexicans live on less than $2 a day, and many more live in dire need. A drive through the low-income municipality of Chimalhuacan (adjacent to Mexico City) and an interview with a destitute family that survives by scavenging a garbage dump in the area show in a way that statistics cannot that Mexico has a long, long way to go before it gives all its people an opportunity to earn a decent standard of living. The municipality depends on water supplied by truck. It has virtually no paved roads, and its sewage is discarded by means of an open, stinking ditch in which people must wash their clothes. How long will it take *FAIS* to satisfy the infrastructure needs of Chimalhuacan and the other 2,424 municipalities of Mexico?

CONCLUSION

In the ideal world, the optimum degree of decentralization is "devolution" in which the center "devolves" to lower levels of government the authority and the means to provide the basic goods and services, the benefits of which correspond to their respective jurisdictions. Because the welfare-maximizing distribution of income exists, each level of government taxes and spends according to the demands of its citizens. Voice, client power and compact are all strong. All levels of government have the administrative capacity to fulfill their responsibilities.

The real world is not ideal. In Mexico and the rest of Latin America, poverty and inequality are extreme. The voice and the client power of the poor are weak to nonexistent. Compacts lack planning and sufficient finance. Administrative capacity is often lacking. The challenging question for decentralization is: Where do we go from here?

Mexico has made a start in developing a decentralization process that contributes to the satisfaction of the basic needs of the poor in a short period of time. The strongest point of the process is the potential for Mexican decentralization to achieve the redistribution of income required to satisfy basic needs soon and to generate an inclusive development process. The potential for redistribution has not been actively exploited, but it is there.

The weakest part of Mexican decentralization is the lack of a comprehensive, coherent plan to satisfy the basic needs of the poor in a short time. Instead of being based on a comprehensive plan, the decentralization process was constructed in a piecemeal fashion. Satisfying basic needs is more of an afterthought in the decentralization process than a central objective. It is more of a concession and an add-on than an integral part of a development plan.

FAIS is a good program that is firmly in place. Perhaps the next step in the evolution of the Mexican decentralization process should be to broaden *FAIS*. Other basic goods and services that are necessary to enhance the productivity of the poor should be included in the program. This could be done by coordinating with other programs such as *Oportunidades* (Chapter 6), or by consolidating other programs with *FAIS*. The financial commitment to satisfying basic needs should be enlarged. The redistribution of income associated with the grant could be strengthened by increasing the progressivity of the tax system and by increasing the size of the fund. Broadening *FAIS* will require not only that the federal government "get serious" about planning and financial commitment, but also that the administrative capacity of municipalities (and, to a lesser extent, of states) be developed.

NOTES

1. The main sources of tax revenues for the states are payroll taxes, annual taxes on automobiles and fees (Giugale & Webb, 2000, p. 16). The main sources of tax revenues for municipalities are property taxes and water-user charges (Giugale & Webb, 2000, p.17).
2. The original derivation principle stipulated that no state should receive less from *participaciones* than they were collecting before joining the revenue-sharing system (Giugale & Webb, 2000, p. 208).

CHAPTER 6

OPORTUNIDADES FOR EDUCATION, HEALTH, AND NUTRITION

"It's the cost of living, low salaries, and lack of jobs. And it's also not having medicine, food, and clothes."

—Indigent Person of Brazil

INTRODUCTION[1]

In 1997, Mexico introduced a new approach to satisfying basic needs that has been found to be effective. The program, called *Oportunidades* (originally *Progresa*) delivers a package of education, health and nutrition benefits to "extremely poor" households of rural and semirural areas.

As of 2009, *Oportunidades* covers approximately 5.1 million families. The program operates in almost 96,000 localities in 2,445 municipalities and in all 31 states plus Mexico City. The budget of *Oportunidades* is approximately $41 bi pesos (approximately 3.1 billion U.S. dollars) (Secretaría de Desarrollo Social [SEDESOL], 2009a).

The program has been—and continues to be—evaluated by a range of external institutions.[2] An outstanding evaluation of the program by International Food Policy Research Institute (IFPRI) concluded that the pro-

Decentralization for Satisfying Basic Needs: An Economic Guide for Policymakers, 2nd Edition
pp. 69–82

gram, as it existed before 2001, was significantly enhancing the education, health and nutrition of the extremely poor at a relatively low cost. As a result, Brazil and other countries throughout Latin America are imitating it.

The stated objective of the program is to "develop the capacities of families living in extreme poverty" (SEDESOL, 2009b, p. 3). The means of accomplishing this objective is to encourage "extremely poor" families of rural and semi-rural areas to invest in education, health and nutrition.

The purpose of this chapter is to draw lessons from the *Oportunidades* program for using decentralization to satisfy the basic needs of the poor. In the first part of the chapter, the program is described. In part two, it is evaluated in light of the decentralization model of chapters 3-4. The chapter concludes with recommendations for policymakers.

OPORTUNIDADES PROGRAM

Selection of Beneficiaries

Oportunidades "targets" extremely poor people living in rural areas. The selection of beneficiaries takes place through a three stage process. The first stage is to identify marginal rural *localities* where the extremely poor are most likely to be found. The regions are identified using a specially constructed "marginality index" based mainly on poverty data from the national census. Additional considerations include locality size (localities with less than 50 and more than 2,500 inhabitants are excluded), and access to some supporting infrastructure such as the presence of a primary school within the locality and access to a secondary school and a health clinic within a certain distance from the locality (Skoufias, 2001, p. 42). In specific cases, some zones of extreme poverty are identified within broader localities that have low levels of marginalization.

The second stage involves identifying households within the eligible localities. The selection of beneficiary families is based on an analysis of extensive socioeconomic information about each household in the selected marginalized community. This information is obtained through a household questionnaire that is designed for this purpose.

After gathering the socioeconomic data through the household survey, a first approximation to the families who live in extreme poverty is made using family income and a poverty line. Income from all sources earned by household members over 15 years of age is compared to a poverty line determined by the cost of a basic food basket that satisfies the minimum requirements for preventing malnutrition, diseases and anthropometric deficiencies. An expansion factor is applied to this cost to take into account minimum irreducible expenditures on nonfood items. This extreme poverty line is adjusted for inflation using the National Consumer Price Index, published by the Bank of Mexico (Skoufias, Davis, & Behrman, 1999, p. 38).

A second classification is then carried out using other socioeconomic indicators derived from the household questionnaire. The purpose is to construct a multidimensional approximation to the poverty condition. A "discriminant analysis" is used, through which it is possible to classify a household as either "in extreme poverty" or "not in extreme poverty" (Skoufias, Davis, & Behrman, 1999, p. 38).

In the third stage, the list of potential beneficiaries is presented to community assemblies for review and discussion. The list is changed according to the established criteria for the selection of beneficiary families. Reportedly, few changes are made at this stage.

Education Benefits and Requirements

The education component of *Oportunidades* provides monetary grants to extremely poor children of marginal rural localities between the ages of 7 and 22 who enroll in school and maintain at least an 85% attendance record, both monthly and annually.[3] The grants provide a new opportunity for extremely poor children to attend school by making it more affordable to families who have difficulty in paying the direct costs of education as well as the indirect costs of foregone earnings of the children while they are in school.

Table 6.1 lists the amounts of the monetary grants for education in 2009. Benefits are adjusted every six months to account for inflation. The grants rise with the grade level, presumably to account for increases in children's earnings as they grow older.

Mexico's children typically maintain a high enrollment rate in primary school (Grades 1-6) of about 93% (Skoufias, 2001, p. 48). For the rural poor, however, education often stops there. The most critical objective of the education program is to increase the transition of poor rural youth into secondary and high school. To achieve this objective, educational grants for enrolling in higher levels of schooling increase substantially. Grants to girls in secondary school are larger than those given to boys in order to counter a relatively high dropout rate, and because women play a critical role in the management of households. Total benefits are limited to 1,1455 pesos per month for families with children in primary and secondary schools, and to 2,345 pesos per month for families with children in primary, secondary and high schools (SEDESOL, 2009a).

Another education program called *Jovenes en Oportunidades* grants additional financial incentives for youth who are in the *Oportunidades* pro-

Table 6.1. Education Benefits of *Oportunidades*, 2009 (Pesos/Month)

Education Scholarships	*Boys*	*Girls*
Primary		
Grade 3	140	140
Grade 4	165	165
Grade 5	210	210
Grade 6	280	280
Materials (annual)	265	265
Secondary		
Grade 7	410	430
Grade 8	430	475
Grade 9	455	525
Materials (annual)	330	330
High School		
Grade 10	685	790
Grade 11	735	840
Grade 12	780	890
Materials	330	330

Source: SEDESOL (2009a).

gram to complete High School before reaching the age of 22 (SEDESOL, 2009c). Starting in the 9th grade, students begin accumulating 3,000 points that entitle them to access a monetary bonus for completing High School. After accumulating 3,000 points, money is deposited in a bank savings account in their name. The peso value of a point changes annually. For the 2007-2008 school year, each point was worth 1.20 pesos. Consequently, an *Oportunidades* student who graduated from high school in 2008 received 3,600 pesos, or about $275. In the very poor states of Chiapas, Sonora and in parts of Vera Cruz, students receive partial payments in advance in order to defer part of the cost of going to school. In order to receive the money, principals and teachers must certify that the students have in fact completed high school.

Health and Nutrition Benefits and Requirements

Table 6.2 lists six interrelated components of the health and nutrition benefits. Emphasis is placed on preventive health care as evidenced in the

Table 6.2. Health and Nutrition Benefits

- Check-up visits to health center
- Health services
- Improved supply of health services
- Food grant
- Nutritional supplement
- Health and nutrition education

Source: Author's summary of Skoufias (2001, Chapter 1).

check-up visits, nutrition aid, and health and nutrition education. While the general focus is on improving the health and nutritional status of all household members, emphasis is placed on the welfare of mothers and children.

Health Care

A crucial ingredient of preventive health care is to require regular visits to health centers as a condition for receiving benefits. A schedule of visits is established for each household, and the visits must be made in order to remain eligible for program benefits. Compliance with the schedule is certified by the doctor or nurse at the clinic. Table 6.3 lists the schedule of visits.

The health centers provide a range of basic services to prevent illness or to treat illnesses that may be discovered during the visits. The services include vaccinations, antiparasite treatment, treatment of respiratory infections, control of tuberculosis, control of high blood pressure and dia-

Table 6.3. Frequency of Health Visits

Age Group	*Annual Frequency*
Children	
Newborn to 1 year of age	7 Check-ups: 7 and 28 days; 2, 4, 6, 9, & 12 months
One to 2 years	4 check-ups: one every three months
Three to 5 years	3 check-ups: one every four months
Six to 11 years	2 check-ups: one every six months
Women	
Of childbearing age	4 check-ups: one every three months
Pregnant	5 check-ups during prenatal period
During puerperium and Lactation	2 check-ups: in immediate puerperium and during lactation
Adults	1 check-up every 12 months

Sources: Coady (2001) and (Skoufias) 2000.

betes mellitus, first aid for injuries, treatment of diarrhea, supervision of children's growth, and so on.

In order to improve the supply of health-care services, resources will be devoted to: (1) ensuring an adequate supply of equipment to units; (2) encouraging staff working in remote rural areas to remain there on a long-term basis; (3) ensuring that health-care units have the necessary medicines and materials; (4) providing extra training to improve both the quality of the medical attention and the operational dimensions of the service.

Nutrition

A monetary transfer for the purchase of food is given to each participating household. In 2009, the transfer was 195 pesos per month; the amount is adjusted regularly for inflation (SEDESOL, 2009d, p. 8). In addition, food supplements are provided to pregnant and lactating women, and to children between the ages of four months and two years. The supplements will also be given to children between two and five years, if any signs of malnutrition are detected, or to non-*Oportunidades* households under similar circumstances.

Two different food supplements were formulated specifically for the program: one for pregnant or lactating women and the other one for young children. The supplements are prepared at one production plant devoted solely to this task and then distributed to health centers. Mothers pick up a one-month supply of the supplement for each targeted household member each month at the health centers.

Health and Nutrition Education

Another crucial element of preventive health care is health and nutrition education. Program participants are required to attend nutrition and health education lectures as another condition for receiving benefits. Twenty-five themes are discussed in the lectures that are directed towards the prevention and recognition of illness and toward following appropriate primary-care procedures. Themes include sanitation at the family level, family planning, prenatal and puerperal care, prevention of diarrhea, accident prevention, and community training for health care self-help. Participants are also trained in the use of a nutritional supplement that is provided by the program, as well as in the optimal feeding of young children.

Other

In addition to the education, health and nutrition benefits described above, *Oportunidades* offers aid to the elderly and aid for paying electricity bills. The elderly who are members of beneficiary families receive 270 pesos each month, and they are entitled to two visits to medical doctors each year. Families who participate in the *Oportunidades* program also receive 50 pesos a month to help pay their energy bills (SEDESOL, 2009d, p. 10).

IMPACT

Education

IFPRI research on the program as it existed before 2001concludes that the main impact of *Oportunidades* on education is to have increased the enrollment in secondary schools more than 20% for girls and 10% for boys (Skoufias, 2001, p. 52). Much of the positive impact on enrollment is due to increasing continuation rates rather than on getting children who were out of school to return.

Health

The health component of *Oportunidades* is clearly having a significant impact. Children 0-5 years of age have a 12% lower incidence of illness than non-*Oportunidades* children. The average beneficiary has 17% fewer days in which he or she is incapacitated by illness (Skoufias, 2001, p. 60). *Oportunidades* increased the number of first visits to health clinics by pregnant women by about 8%, and this has made a significant improvement in the health of babies and pregnant mothers (Skoufias, 2001, p. 56).

Nutrition

The average level of consumption (including purchases and consumption out of own production) increased by approximately 14.53% (Hoddinott et al., 2000; cited in Skoufias, 2001, p. 65). In November, 1999, median food expenditures were 10.6% higher in *Oportunidades* households when compared with comparable control households. The increase in household consumption was driven largely by higher expenditures on fruits, vegetables, meats, and animal products (Skoufias, 2001, p. 59).

In 1998, survey results indicated that 44% of children of the critical 12-36 month age range in *Oportunidades* regions were stunted (low height for age). Stunting is widely perceived to have substantial and persistent impact on children's physical and mental development and on their health status as adults (Skoufias, 2001, p. 59). Children who received treatment during this age range experienced, on average, an increase of

16% in their growth per year. The impact from the nutrition supplements alone could account for a 2.9% increase in lifetime earnings (Behrman & Hoddinott; cited in Skoufias, 2001, p. 63).

In addition there are likely to be other effects through increased cognitive development, increased schooling, and lowered age of completing given levels of schooling through starting when younger and passing grades at a higher rate. Since the nutrition supplement constitutes only a small fraction of the program costs, the benefit to cost ratio of the nutrition supplement is likely to be high.

Poverty

Oportunidades has had an immediate, short-run impact on poverty through monetary transfers and other supports. IFPRI estimates that the supports of the program have reduced poverty by about 10% (Skoufias, 2001, p. 44). The poverty gap (the average difference between actual income and the poverty line) is reduced by 30%, and the largest reductions in poverty are being achieved in the poorest of the poor population.

However, the main impact of *Oportunidades* is likely to be long-term as more educated and healthy children grow and enter the labor force as workers with increased productivity. IFPRI estimates that the increased years of schooling alone will generate permanently higher earnings of 8% (Skoufias, 2001, p. 53). The impact from nutrition supplements that are described below could cause another 2.9% increase in lifetime earnings (Behrman and Hoddinott; cited in Skoufias, 2001, p. 63).

EVALUATION

The *Oportunidades* program makes a significant advance in the planning and implementation of basic needs programs, but there is room for improvement. This section uses the planning model of chapters 3-4 to identify and discuss the strengths and weaknesses of the *Oportunidades* program. Let us consider each element of the planning model in turn.

Degree of Decentralization

Oportunidades is an example of administrative “deconcentration.” Planning and finance are centralized, and delivery is carried out by deconcentrated offices of the central government.

Objective

The program has a clearly defined objective: to "develop the capacities of families living in extreme poverty" by improving the education, health and nutrition of the rural and semirural poor. Education, health and nutrition are crucial for enhancing the productivity of the poor, enabling them to contribute to the development process and to enjoy its fruits. Furthermore, some of the worst poverty exists in rural areas. Limitations of the objective are that it ignores other important goods and services such as housing and sanitation, and no limit is placed upon the time within which the basic needs are to be satisfied.

Beneficiaries

The benefits of *Oportunidades* are laudably targeted to the "extremely poor." The term, "extremely poor," is defined more liberally by Mexico than by the World Bank. According to the World Bank, a person lives in "extreme poverty" if he or she lives on less than $1 per day (PPP 1985 US$). This is the amount of money estimated to be necessary to purchase just the amount of food required in order to survive (Nafziger, 1997, p. 127). Mexico's definition of "extreme poverty" allows for the purchase of both food and some nonfood items.

The authors of the program have devised a sophisticated method of "targeting" benefits to the "extremely poor." The system is to use census data to identify marginalized areas, use a household survey to identify the poor within those areas, and then finalize a preliminary list of beneficiaries in a community assembly. Sophisticated statistical techniques are utilized in the first two stages of the process.

Despite its sophistication, the method of targeting households undoubtedly omits many extremely poor households. One condition for being a beneficiary is that the household must live in localities with more than 50 and less than 2,500 inhabitants, and the localities must have access to health clinics and schools where accessibility is measured in terms of access to roads. Many poor households surely live in localities that fall outside these population limits, and in localities that do not pass the test for access to supporting infrastructure. Other extremely poor people live in areas designated as nonpoor.

Another group of extremely poor who are excluded from receiving the program's benefits are the urban poor. Morley finds that since 1989 more than 50% of Latin America's poor live in urban areas. The poverty line used by Morley is $2 per day, a line that would approximately equal the definition of "extreme poverty" used by *Oportunidades*. According to Mor ley's data, 43% of Mexico's "poor" lived in urban areas in 1989 (Morley, 1995, pp. 36-41). Mexico's SEDESOL recently found that more than half of Mexico's poor live in urban areas. The government is attempting to take this demographic shift into account by expanding the coverage of the program to include families who live in Mexico's largest urban areas (Mexican Economic Report, 2004, p. 3).

An advantage of the targeting technique is that it is cost effective. To search out every poor person in the country who meets the eligibility requirements would be costly, and at some point, the costs would become greater than the benefits. Also, the limitations of the targeting are partially overcome by an escape clause that allows the program to help extremely poor households that are not in the specified "marginal areas," should they be discovered.

Resources

We have seen that *Oportunidades* is currently serving approximately 5 million people. It is estimated that in 2006, 8.7% of Mexicans were living on less than $1 a day, and that the population of Mexico was 105,258,000 (CEPALSTAT, 2009). This implies that about 9.2 million people were living in "extreme poverty." *Oportunidades* is serving little more than one-half the people who are living on less than $1 a day. Furthermore, it is estimated that in 2006, 31.7% of Mexicans were living on less than $2 a day (CEPALSTAT, 2009). *Oportunidades* is serving less than one-sixth of the 33.5 million people living on less than $2 a day. How many more people are living on less than $3, $4, or $5 a day?

Mexico has increased the coverage of *Oportunidades* substantially over the years. The number of families assisted has more than doubled in the last decade, increasing from approximately 2.5 million in 2000 to more than 5 million in 2008. Since beginning the program in 1997, *Oportunidades* has added assistance for the elderly, for helping families pay their energy bills, and for youth attending high school. Still, if Mexico is to eliminate nothing more than extreme poverty in the foreseeable future, it must continue making very substantial increases in the resources dedicated to *Oportunidades*.

Compact: Sectors

The sectors addressed by *Oportunidades* are necessary elements of an effective antipoverty program. Much empirical evidence supports the effectiveness of education in increasing incomes. The classic study that was cited in chapter 2 concluded that the average social rate of return to primary education in Latin America and the Caribbean was 18% (Psacharopoulos, 1994, Table 1, p. 1328). Health and nutrition are obviously necessary in order to learn and to be productive.

Oportunidades does an excellent job of linking three goods and services whose benefits are interrelated. Before *Oportunidades*, government interventions in education, health and nutrition consisted of many separate programs with little prior consideration of the potential synergies that could result from a better coordinated and simultaneous intervention (Skoufias, 2001, p. 8). If the three are not linked, a lack of nutrition could undermine health programs. A lack of health could undermine nutrition programs. A lack of health or nutrition could undermine education programs. Combining the three elements no doubt greatly increases the effectiveness and reduces the costs of antipoverty efforts.

The education and health benefits are carefully designed to maximize their effectiveness. The stipend for attending school that rises with age accounts for the rising opportunity costs of foregone earnings as age increases, and it counters the trend to drop out of school after the sixth grade, especially for girls. The education stipend includes money for school supplies. Very importantly, providing support for education in the form of a cash grant to students does not preclude decentralizing the supply of education to the local level. The health program consists of a package of services that promise to make the program effective including a carefully designed schedule of regular visits and a range of health services. The food program includes not only a monetary stipend, but also a nutritional supplement. The program is topped off with health and nutrition education.

In addition to carefully packaging benefits, steps are taken to ensure that the beneficiaries take full advantage of them. To remain in the program, students must maintain an 85% attendance rate, families must make regular visits to the health clinic, and they must attend the preventive health lectures. The requirements for participation in the program are excellent.

Education, health and nutrition are extremely important goods and services that must be supplied if the poor are to be integrated into the development process. Still, other basic goods and services such as roads, potable water and sewerage are also important.

Supplying the other basic goods and services is left to other programs such as *FAIS* (chapter 5). The Director of *Oportunidades* in the state of Coahuila was asked whether the program was coordinated with others. The response was "No" (C. G. Ramírez Hernández, personal communication, April 4, 2004). Once again, Mexico lacks an over-all, comprehensive plan to satisfy all basic needs of the poor within a short time.

Delivery

Oportunidades has developed a clever mechanism to assure the delivery of its goods and services to the poor. The delivery mechanism is not so much to bring the services to the people, but rather to bring the people to the services. It does this by assuring that beneficiaries have access to the services and by requiring that they take advantage of that access. IFPRI research finds that "the largest reductions in poverty ... are being achieved in the poorest of the poor population" (Skoufias, 2001, p. 44).

Monitoring

The program has been analyzed and found to be effective by many outside experts such as IFPRI, and the SEDESOL web site reports extensive data on expenditures and beneficiaries. Demonstrations of effectiveness are necessary for programs to be widely imitated. Countries are unlikely to commit large amounts of resources to basic needs programs without convincing evidence that they will succeed.

Voice and Client Power

Oportunidades is essentially a top-down program that is planned and executed by central government. The result tends to be weak voice and client power. *Oportunidades* has attempted to counter this tendency by making the authorities available to the program's participants. The SEDESOL web site lists a toll-free telephone number, a mailing address, and an e-mail address that citizens can use to record their observations about the program. In 2007, *Oportunidades* received 82,848 contacts from citizens. Seventy-three percent of the contacts were requests for assistance, and 22.9% were complaints. The large number of comments suggests that contact information is widely distributed by means other than the web page.

Furthermore, *Oportunidades* has formed community promotion committees (*comités de promoción comunitaria*) composed of representatives of the beneficiary families (SEDESOL, 2009e). The function of the committees is to channel petitions and suggestions of the participating families to the personnel of *Oportunidades*, and so improve services. It appears, therefore, that *Oportunidades* is making substantial and laudable efforts to counter the tendency associated with the deconcentration form of decentralization to weaken voice and client power.

Demand Versus Supply

Oportunidades is essentially a demand-side program in the sense that the rural poor are empowered to demand more of the goods and services that exist. With the possible exception of the unspecified commitment to increase the supply of health services, there is limited provision within *Oportunidades* to increase the supply of basic goods and services. The education grants, for example, encourage more students to attend existing schools. The burning question is: at what point does the existing supply become overwhelmed? At some point, growth in demand will exhaust the existing supply, and it will be necessary to turn attention to increasing the supply of the services. An open question is whether the supply of health and other services will be increased sufficiently. One feature of the program helps to obviate this problem: the emphasis on preventive medicine through health and nutrition education.

Increasing the supply of basic goods and services is left to other programs such as *FAIS* (chapter 5). Is the supply of basic goods and services by other programs coordinated with the demand created by the beneficiaries of *Oportunidades*? The director of *Oportunidades* in Chihuahua commented that they are not (C. G. Ramírez Hernández, personal communication, April 4, 2004).

CONCLUSION

Overall, *Oportunidades* is an excellent program that constitutes a fundamental advance in programs for satisfying the basic needs of the poor. It supplies three basic goods and services that are crucial for integrating the extremely poor of rural areas into the development process, education, health and nutrition. It is innovative in linking the three goods and services in a way that takes advantage of their synergies. The supply of each sector is brilliantly designed. Program requirements help to assure that beneficiaries take advantage of their opportunities. The government has made a substantial financial commitment to implementing the program. The program has been scientifically monitored by highly qualified experts who conclude that the benefits arrive to the poorest of the poor, and that the program is indeed effective. Steps have been taken to increase the participation of beneficiaries in the satisfaction of their basic needs.

Despite its many strengths, *Oportunidades* benefits a limited subset of Mexico's poor. Moreover, some important basic needs are not included in the *Oportunidades* program. In order to satisfy all the basic needs that incorporate every person into the development process, Mexico's financial commitment must be multiplied. Similar needs exist throughout Latin America. This raises the question of international aid by the United States to Latin America and other developing countries. We turn to this topic in chapter 10.

Oportunidades is an example of administrative "deconcentration" in which planning and financing are centralized, and in which the benefits are delivered by deconcentrated offices of the central government. The great strength is that a highly rational package of services has been developed and delivered to the extremely poor of rural areas. In terms of the decentralization model, the compact is very strong. The achievements in improving the education, health and nutrition of the poor can have lasting consequences on their contribution to development and their earning power in the future.

The main weakness of deconcentration is that it results in weak voice and client power. *Oportunidades* has made significant strides to overcome this weakness by establishing an agency to receive comments, and by establishing the community promotion committees. The ongoing challenge will be to use the comments to generate continual improvements in the program.

NOTES

1. The description of *Oportunidades* is derived mainly from Skoufias, 2001, and from the SEDESOL web site.
2. Prestigious institutions that have evaluated *Oportunidades* include Centro de Investigación y Docencia Económica (CIDE), the International Food Policy Research Institute (IFPRI), El Colegio de México (COLMEX), el Instituto Nacional de Salud Pública (INSP), el Centro de Investigación y Estudios Superiores en Antropología Social (CIESAS), the University of Pennsylvania, the University of California, Berkeley, and the Massachusetts Institute of Technology (MIT). Many of the evaluation documents are available online (SEDESOL, 2009b)
3. A student loses the educational grant for the month in which he or she has four unexcused absences. A student who has 12 or more unexcused absences in a semester loses the grant for the rest of the semester. A student who registers three times for the same grade loses the grant until he or she passes that grade (SEDESOL, 2009c, p. 35).

CHAPTER 7

COMMUNITY GOVERNMENT IN TLAXCALA

"For the poor, empowerment, security, and opportunity must all be experienced at the local level."

—Narayan, Patel, Schafft, Rademacher, and Koch-Schulte (2000)

INTRODUCTION

The state of Tlaxcala, Mexico, has taken a unique and intensely interesting approach to decentralization. It has brought government closer to the people, not by decentralizing the taxing and spending powers to its states and municipalities, but rather by creating a whole new fourth level of government, called community governments (*presidencias municipales comunitarias*). In terms of Figure 4.1, this "quiet revolution" has generated three levels of subnational governments: the state (*estado*), the municipality (*municipalidad*) and the community government (*presidencia municipal comunitaria*).

The new community governments have been given full legal status in the state constitution. Legally, they are subordinate to their municipalities in the sense that their first responsibilities are to represent the community to the municipality and to carry out the resolutions of city hall (*municipalidad*). At the same time, the community governments enjoy considerable

Decentralization for Satisfying Basic Needs: An Economic Guide for Policymakers, 2nd Edition
pp. 83–100

autonomy. They elect their own authorities. They identify and prioritize their own needs for public services, they plan their own social development projects, and they receive the federal *FAIS* grants (described in chapter 5) which they use to carry out their planned projects.

The purpose of this chapter is to describe Tlaxcala's unique approach to decentralization and to evaluate it in terms of its ability to satisfy the basic needs of the poor. In section one, the historical evolution of the state's decentralization process is described. Section two describes the process of using *FAIS* money to satisfy the basic needs of the poor. Section three evaluates Tlaxcala's approach to decentralization as a means of satisfying basic needs in light of the decentralization model of chapters 2-3. The chapter concludes with recommendations for policymakers.

EVOLUTION OF TLAXCALA'S DECENTRALIZATION PROCESS[1]

Tlaxcala's process of decentralization has evolved in five stages. The purpose of this section is to describe that evolution and so to give a practical feel for what is required politically and economically for decentralization to progress over time. We will see that economic and political factors drove the process.

Stage 1: Centralization

After the conquest of Mexico in the 1500s, the Spanish established a highly centralized governmental structure that was designed to control and exploit the natives. Municipalities were a part of that structure.

More specifically, municipalities were a centralized means of enforcing two mechanisms of control, the *repartimiento* and the *encomienda*. The *repartimiento* was territory that was assigned to the conquistador. The *encomienda* was the number of natives assigned to serve him. Municipal governments were structured to enforce these mechanisms. Membership on the city council (*ayuntamiento*) was limited to the *conquistadores,* and later to their sons, the *criollos*. City council consisted of "municipal agents" (*agentes municipales* or *delegados municipales*) who were appointed and whose primary responsibility was to carry out the resolutions of the municipality in their communities. The law and police force were other variables in the formula.

Neither the revolution of 1810 nor that of 1910 broke this structure of domination. After the revolutions, the municipality remained a highly centralized mechanism for maintaining "internal colonization." City council was represented in the community, but the community was virtually unrepresented in city council.

Stage 2: Elections of Municipal Agents

In 1868, Tlaxcala took its first step toward decentralization by instituting elections of municipal agents. Henceforward, these members of city council were to be elected by their communities rather than be appointed by the city council. This gave some voice to the people. Since they were required to win elections, the agents necessarily assumed a secondary role of representing the people to the council. However, the voice of the people was often captured by local elites, and the primary function of municipal agents remained much the same: carry out the resolutions of city council in the communities. This took the forms of keeping public order, informing the mayor of "notable occurrences," and maintaining roads and other infrastructure.

Stage 3: Municipal Agents as Community Representatives

In 1984, under the leadership of Governor Tulio Hernández, the state government revised municipal law (*ley orgánica municipal*) in order to strengthen the representation of communities in city council. To symbolize the change in emphasis, the municipal agent was renamed "*regidor de pueblo*" ("leader of the people").

The primary role of the *regidor* was now to be an elected representative of his or her community who serves as a member of city council with a voice and vote in policymaking. Hence, the primary role of the city council person shifted dramatically from representing the city to the community, to representing the community to the city.

The *regidor* was assigned new responsibilities that reflected this change in emphasis. The new role of the city council person was redefined to: (1) represent the community in the city council; (2) carry out the resolutions of the city council in the community; (3) promote the participation and cooperation of the people in programs that benefit their community; and (4) administer and collect the property tax (Olmedo Carranza, 1999, pp. 83-84).

Stage 4: School of Democracy

The next 10 years, 1984-1994, served as a school of democracy for the communities of Tlaxcala. The *regidores* learned to debate, negotiate, analyze and manage political forces. In short, they learned to govern. During the course of the decade, communities came to realize that they were capable of governing themselves, and many came to believe that they could govern themselves better than their municipality.

Stage 5: Community Governments

Political and Economic Causes

By 1994, the communities of Tlaxcala had gained voice and vote in city council, but a serious lack of representation remained that was a byproduct of the colonial period. The underrepresentation was caused by the limited number of municipalities that exist in Mexico.

In Mexico, there are 2,457 subnational government units (2,425 municipalities and 32 states including the federal district). In contrast, there are 83,000 government units in the United States, and 47,000 in France. Mexico's population of 104 million is about one third that of the United States, and about twice that of France. If Mexico's governmental structure were like that of the United States, it would have more than 27,500 units of government, not 2,457. If it were like France, it would have 94,000 units of government.

The small number of municipalities in Mexico means that they tend to be large conglomerations of many communities, each of which tends to be under-represented. It is difficult to be heard by a large and distant municipal government that has the responsibility of serving many communities. Some communities had gone 20 years without communicating with their municipality, and had lived virtually independently of them (Olmedo Carranza, 1999, p.96). Olmedo Carranza comments that the number of municipalities that was established by the Spanish after the conquest was deliberately small precisely in order to deprive people of voice, and to make it easier to dominate them (Olmedo Carranza, 1999, pp. 87-88).

Another problem was economic in nature. The proportion of the state's gross domestic product produced by industry had fallen from 42% in 1990 to 35% in 1995. Imports were hurting Tlaxcala's agricultural sector. Most of the new businesses were assembly plants (*maquiladoras*) that were having little multiplier effect and were unstable investments (plan estatal, "diagnóstico").

The communities of Tlaxcala had learned to govern themselves. Despite their advances, they were underrepresented, and they were suffering economic hard times. The political and economic realities reinforced the growing belief in communities that they would be better off if they were independent municipalities.

New Municipalities

Consequently in 1994, communities began to demand the right to become independent municipalities with their own city councils and their own resources. The candidate for governor, José Antonio Álvarez Lima, took note of the movement during his political campaign.

In 1995, the community, Santa Apolonia Teacalco, became verbally and physically violent with its *regidor* for failing to attend to its demand to be made an independent municipality. Soon, other communities began to make similar protests.

However, there was a legal obstacle to forming more municipalities. It was that the state constitution had two requirements that a community must meet in order to become a municipality: (1) it must have at least 30,000 inhabitants; and (2) it must be economically self-sufficient. None of the communities that wanted to become municipalities met these prerequisites.

The new Governor José Antonio Álvarez Lima and the state congress responded to the civic unrest by substituting 22 new requirements for the two that were prohibiting communities from forming new municipalities (Constitución Política, Artículo 21). In terms of satisfying the basic needs of the poor, the requirements included: (1) having a development plan; (2) having the capacity to provide basic transportation, health and education services; (3) having the ability to carry out public works projects; and (4) being able to manage public finance. The new requirements led to the creation of 16 new municipalities.

The good news was that some communities had their desires to be elevated to the level of a municipality satisfied—16 new municipalities were formed. The bad news was that the average size of the new municipalities was a very small 3,537 inhabitants, and, despite a requirement that they be so, not all of the municipalities were economically self-sufficient. The viability of some depended upon state and federal government aid, and this required a restructuring of state finance. Also, some of the municipalities from which the new governments were carved objected to the loss of their territory and their citizens.

New Community Governments

These forces and counter-forces led the state to take the bold and creative step of creating a fourth level of government, community governments (*presidencias municipales comunitarias*). In 1995, no less than four hundred traditional communities of Tlaxcala were legally constituted as community governments. This dramatically changed the structure of Tlaxcala's government. In 1985, there were 45 units of government in Tlaxcala (the state and 44 municipalities). Ten years later, in 1995, there were 461 units of government (the state, 60 municipalities and 400 Community Governments).

Governance

Article 87 of the State Constitution states that communities will be led by community presidents (*presidentes municipales comunitarios*) who are elected for 3-year terms by the communities that they serve, and who are full-fledged members of city council: City councils will consist of a municipal president (*presidente municipal* or mayor), a city manager (*síndico*), council persons (*regidores*), and community presidents (*presidentes municipales comunitarios*). The candidates for community president are to participate in the same election as the other members of city council, and, like the other council members, they cannot be elected for two successive terms (Constitución Política, Artículo 87).

Article 56 of State Law for Municipalities details 22 rights and duties of the community presidents (Ley Orgánica, Artículo 56). Most importantly, from the point of view of satisfying the basic needs of the poor, the community president must attend the meetings of city council; plan and carry out public works projects; report to the city council every month on the progress of projects; collect the property tax if the community has been certified as having the administrative capacity to do so; promote the participation and cooperation of residents in programs that benefit the community; and form a potable water commission.

Article 94 of the State Constitution declares that the community presidents will form "committees of public works and material resources," and that the presidents "will publish in the Official Bulletin the distribution that is made of its resources" (Constitución Política, Artículo 94).

Relation to Municipalities

Article 87 of the State Constitution declares that community governments are not independent, autonomous units of government, but rather branches of the municipalities to which they pertain: "Community governments are deconcentrated branches of the Municipal Government, subordinate to the city council of which it is a part, ... , and they will act in their respective jurisdictions as representatives of the same" (Constitución Política, Artículo 87).

Nevertheless, as noted above, communities do enjoy autonomy. They elect their own representatives, they receive federal funding, and they plan and carry out their own development projects. Olmedo Carranza comments that in fact they are more like "small municipalities" than deconcentrated offices of the municipal government (Olmedo Carranza, 1999, p. 116).

Minimum Conditions

Tlaxcala's State Law for Municipalities details three simple requirements for forming a community government. Article 49 states that the area that wishes to form a community government must contain at least 1,000 residents. Article 50 requires the community to possess "sufficient capacity to offer minimal municipal services," to provide office space for the community government, and to have at least one hectare (2.5 acres) of land for a cemetery (Ley Orgánica, Artículos 49-50). The State Congress declares an area a community government at the behest of the municipality to which it belongs.

DELIVERING SOCIAL INFRASTRUCTURE TO THE POOR[2]

Tlaxcala has decentralized the satisfaction of basic needs by creating a new fourth level of government, the community government, and by redistributing responsibilities for satisfying the basic needs of the poor among the three subnational governments, the state, the municipality and the community. The purpose of this section is to describe the role of community governments in spending the federal *FAIS* grant for providing social infrastructure to the poor. The following section will use the decentralization model of chapters 3-4 to evaluate the effectiveness of Tlaxcala's decentralization in implementing a basic needs approach to development.

Agencies and Their Roles

In the state of Tlaxcala, all three levels of subnational government (state, municipal and community) influence the community's role in delivering social infrastructure to the poor, and there are two institutions at each level of government. At the level of the state, there are the state congress and the state planning committee, COPLADET (*Comité de Planeación del Estado de Tlaxcala*). At the level of the municipality, there are the city council and the municipal planning agency, called the municipal development council (*consejo de desarrollo municipal*). At the level of the community, there are the community committee (*comité comunitario*), and the public works committee (*comité de obra*).

The State Congress and COPLADET

The state and its planning commission, COPLADET, establish state priorities and general guidelines for the use of federal social development grants. As indicated in the last chapter, almost all federal grants are distributed first to the states and from there to the municipalities. Municipal (and community) development plans must conform to these priorities and guidelines in order to receive funds from the state government.

In the state of Tlaxcala, a very simple formula is used to distribute *FAIS* money from the state to its municipalities and communities: money is distributed on an equal per capita basis with the exception that 20% of the money is assigned according to the degree of community poverty (Olmedo Carranza, 1999, p. 156).

The Municipality

The municipal development council, with the approval of its city council, establishes municipal guidelines for the use of the *FAIS* development funds by its communities. The municipal guidelines must conform to the state and national guidelines. The municipal development council also promotes the formation of the community committees that are described below, and it monitors and evaluates the use of the funds that the community committees spend.

The Community

Every community government is required to establish a community committee (*comité comunitario*). Its membership consists of the community president (*presidente municipal comunitario*) and six community advisors (*consejeros comunitarios*) who are elected democratically in a public assembly. All members of the community committee serve without remuneration (Olmedo Carranza, 1999, p. 141).

The community committee prioritizes the demands of the community in accord with the limits of its budget. It does so by first conducting and publishing a study of the community, called the "integral perspective of the community" (*perspectiva integral de la comunidad*). The study identifies needs and serves as the basis for proposing priorities and alternative possible solutions. After conducting the study, the committee presents a list of preliminary recommendations for community development projects to a general assembly for discussion, revision and approval.

The other important institution on the community level is the public works committee (*comité de obra*). A distinct public works committee is instituted for each development project. The role of the public works committee is to manage the one project for which it was created. It manages both the resources and the construction of the project. It also foments the participation of the community beneficiaries in constructing the project. Once the project is completed, the committee goes out of existence. The formation of a public works committee is a prerequisite for receiving state funds.

The public works committee consists of a president, a secretary, a treasurer, two community representatives and a comptroller, all of whom are elected democratically in a community assembly. In addition, persons in the community who have special skills needed to carry out a particular project may also serve on the committee. Again, all members serve without remuneration.

Three-Stage Implementation

Development projects are implemented in three stages. First, the community committee conducts its study of community needs and convokes the general assembly in which a list of potential development projects is finalized. The community committee then presents the proposals to the municipality's planning agency, the municipal development council, for evaluation and approval. The city council considers the recommendations of the municipal development council, makes any adjustments that may be necessary to coordinate with municipal, state and national plans, and authorizes the projects.

In the second stage, the municipality informs the citizens about the nature and location of the projects, and the plans to complete them. It details the beneficiaries and their responsibilities to participate in the construction of the projects. It names the persons in charge, and it establishes the dates for beginning and completing the projects. The community is notified by posters that are placed in public places.

In stage three, each public works committee manages the project for which it was created. The committee reports regularly to community assemblies about the progress of its project, and its use of money and materials. It also gives an account of its expenditures to the municipal government, which in turn reports to the state. The state reports to the Federal Government.

EVALUATION

The purpose of this section is to evaluate the role of Tlaxcala's community governments in satisfying the basic needs of the poor and implementing a basic needs approach to development. First, we will use the model of chapters 3-4 to identify the principle strengths of the state's style of decentralization, and then we will consider some issues associated with creating community governments.

Degree of Decentralization

We have seen that legally, the community governments are "deconcentrated" branches of the municipality, but in reality they are legal, permanent government entities with their own budgets and with the autonomy to elect their own authorities, and to initiate and implement their own development plans.

Using Table 4.1, Tlaxcala's decentralization can be categorized as "delegation." Political delegation exists because the community authorities are elected locally and have substantial autonomy, but they are partially accountable to higher levels of government. Fiscal delegation exists because community governments have extensive authority over the expenditure of funds, but most funds come from the center, and general spending priorities and norms are set by the center. Administrative delegation exists because community governments "employ" and manage their own staff, but the state requires that community officials will serve without remuneration, and development plans must conform to state and federal criteria.

Voice and Client Power

The clearest and one of the most important strengths of Tlaxcala's form of decentralization is to greatly strengthen the voice and client power of the "voiceless" poor. Voice is strengthened by relatively small communities electing community presidents who are familiar with the distinctive needs of their areas and who represent those needs to their municipalities as full-fledged city council persons with the power of voice and vote. Contrast the voice of full membership on city council with that of sending a petition to city hall, or of serving on a volunteer committee. Voice is further strengthened by electing (or serving on) the community committees that identify and prioritize unsatisfied basic needs, and by community assemblies that revise and approve the list of development projects proposed by the community committees.

Voice has been strengthened still more by community governments shifting the balance of power from the federal to municipal governments. Traditionally, the federal government held the majority of seats on city planning agencies, the municipal development councils. This arrangement has been heavily criticized for enabling the federal government to use its majority position to direct the use of funds to serve political purposes rather than to satisfy pressing social needs (Olmedo Carranza, 1999, p. 150). At best, the federal government used its majority to dictate development policy to the municipalities in a top-down fashion.

The new political structure has placed enough community presidents on the municipal development councils to give municipal governments a majority of seats and control over planning. Decentralized planning has replaced centralized planning.

Tlaxcala's new political structure not only strengthens the voice of the poor. It also gives them much more client power over the providers of public goods and services. Client power is strengthened through electing (or serving on) the public works committees that manage development projects. It is strengthened through responding in community assemblies to reports on the progress of projects by public works committees. It is strengthened again through the participation of the beneficiaries in the construction of their projects. It is strengthened yet again by empowering clients to monitor projects through publishing a full range of information on their distribution, progress and outcomes.

Participation

Community governments greatly increase the active participation of community members in the development process. Citizens who were once passive recipients of whatever came (or did not come) from on high, are transformed into dynamic subjects who determine their own destinies. They think. They plan. They discuss. They serve as president or committee members. They vote to elect their president and their committees. They vote on development plans. They participate in the construction of their own projects. They come alive and organize to build their own communities.

Two of the greatest afflictions of poverty and underdevelopment are to be voiceless and powerless. The Tlaxcala decentralization by creating a fourth level of government appears to make a very important contribution to overcoming these afflictions. The community governments of Tlaxcala offer policymakers a very interesting model of how to strengthen the voice and the power of the poor through decentralization.

Leadership

One sees in the history of Tlaxcala the importance of leadership for advancing in the process of decentralization. The new structure of government depended heavily on the extraordinary leadership of the state's governors during the 1984-1994 decade and beyond. Less skillful politicians might have appealed to the state constitution and simply suppressed the civic unrest over the failure to designate new municipalities.

Instead, the governor listened, created a bold plan to restructure the political system, and led the state congress to implement the plan. People can voice their preferences, but in the end, there has to be someone there to listen and to respond creatively. If the state leadership is weak, demands crafted skillfully by the citizens imitating the Tlaxcala model may help to compensate.

Mutual Benefits

Politically, all parties seem to have enjoyed significant benefits from the new political arrangement that was adopted in Tlaxcala. The burden (or over-burden) of federal, state and municipal governance was lightened by decentralizing responsibilities for combating poverty to the community level, and by marshaling an army of new resources to contribute to that struggle. Communities gained a new opportunity to develop by receiving more federal money, and more power to use that money to satisfy the basic needs that they consider most pressing. Recognizing the win-win outcome can help policymakers advance the agenda of creating more units of government.

The Indigenous

The new structure of government has given indigenous communities legal autonomy to govern their own communities in accord with their ancient customs. Instead of being awkward exceptions to the rule, the new structure makes room for them to maintain their traditional forms of governance and to fit more comfortably into the over-all political and economic systems. This can dissipate tensions between the indigenous and higher levels of government.

Decentralization is a Process

Decentralization in Tlaxcala has been an evolutionary process, each stage of which provided experience and preparation for the following stage. It would have been difficult to leap directly from highly centralized municipalities designed to exploit people to autonomous community governments. In principle, a good approach for policymakers is to assess the current capacity of the community and to make a prudent judgment about the possibilities for advancing. Attentive listening to the voice of the people may be the best indicator of being ready to advance.

Some Issues

Despite its great strengths, the Tlaxcala decentralization is not without its issues. Recognizing and dealing with them can help Tlaxcala's decentralization to evolve into a more effective form, and it can help others to derive from the Tlaxcala experience more useful styles of decentralization.

Costs

Tlaxcala went from 45 to 461 units of government in a short period of time. This marks a 900% increase in the number of governmental units within the state. The average size of the new municipalities was 3,537 inhabitants, and communities may have as few as 1,000 inhabitants. Is it cost effective to create so many new, and such small, units of government?

Economic theory teaches that the optimum number of governments depends not only on the benefits of decentralization, but also upon the costs (Oates, 1972, pp. 38-45). The benefits of more (and smaller) jurisdictions include tailoring the supply of public goods and services to meet the distinctive preferences of their citizens, the poor becoming subjects of their own destinies and overcoming neglect by municipal governments. On the other hand, more units can increase the cost-per-person of supplying public goods and services.

Important economies of scale in providing public goods and services may exist, that is, the cost-per-person of public goods and services may fall as the size of the jurisdiction increases. Is it cost effective for each of 400 communities—that can have as few as 1,000 residents—to carry out its own public works projects and to have its own police force? At what point does the multiplication of public administrations become inefficient? Is it efficient to employ a staff or purchase buildings and equipment for an additional 400 community governments?

Tlaxcala has partially side-stepped the costs of personnel in money terms (but not in real terms) by requiring that community officials serve without remuneration. Indeed, this provision may be necessary for making its decentralization financially viable. Costs are also reduced by generating the voluntary participation of previously idle community members in planning and constructing their projects.

It is difficult to make an a priori judgment about the net effect of Tlaxcala's decentralization on the costs of its public goods and services. Nevertheless, the message is that policymakers must consider costs as well as benefits in determining the number of subnational governments. In principle, they must limit the number of subnational governments to the number that maximizes the excess of benefits over costs.

Correspondence

The theory of fiscal federalism teaches that the welfare is maximized by a "correspondence" between the governmental jurisdictions and the areas containing the beneficiaries of public goods and services. If some beneficiaries live outside the jurisdiction, "external benefits" exist. If the community fails to consider the external benefits, under-supply will result. If "external costs" exist, over-supply can occur.

State policymakers should take into account this principle of correspondence in forming new units of government. Either the jurisdiction that supplies public goods and services should be adjusted so that it encompasses the beneficiaries, or the responsibilities of community governments for supplying goods and services should be limited so that the principle of correspondence is honored.

Did the State of Tlaxcala consider the principle of correspondence when it determined the number of new municipalities and community governments? Our brief history of the decentralization process suggests that the principle motive driving the government to form the community governments was to quell civic unrest. It seems unlikely that correspondence (or for that matter costs) was carefully considered when the State established in one fell swoop the "400 traditional communities" of Tlaxcala as community governments. The potentially small size of the new community governments, together with the nature of the social infrastructure projects for which they are responsible, suggests that the principle of correspondence was not always honored.

Dependence on Volunteers

The State Law for Municipalities details a long list of responsibilities for community presidents that are serving without remuneration. They are charged with 22 responsibilities ranging from attending the meetings of city council, to serving on community committees, to maintaining the cadastre of property values, to collecting the property tax for the municipalities. The list reads like a full time job description. Likewise the community committees that identify community needs and the public works committees that manage development projects are assigned heavy responsibilities.

On the one hand, the volunteers have the motivation that comes from knowing that their services directly benefit their own communities. Also, Mexican culture is such that the volunteers view their public service as a "distinction and honor" (Olmedo Carranza, 1999, p. 141). On the other hand, how much can be expected from volunteer labor? Policymakers need to be realistic in assigning responsibilities to community volunteers.

Administrative Capacity

The new structure of government in Tlaxcala places a lot of responsibility on small communities to plan and carry out projects. A question arises about their capacity to meet that responsibility. We saw in chapter 5 that the majority of Mexican municipalities suffer from severe administrative shortcomings. If the municipalities lack administrative capacity, what must be the lack among the communities?

When the creation of the community governments was being debated by the state congress, one of the arguments against creating them was that they lacked the administrative ability to carry out their proposed functions. It was argued that many community governments would split up the few capable administrators that existed on the municipal level and lower the quality of municipal administration even further (Olmedo Carranza, 1999, pp. 100-101).

In response, Governor José Antonio Álvarez Lima argued not only that the quality of administration would not be harmed, but that it would indeed be improved. He argued that the people were enthusiastic about the new opportunities to develop their own communities, and that there is no substitute for enthusiasm. He said that improved representation (voice and client power) would improve administration. Projects would be planned and carried out where they are most needed. He said that the great failure of public administration in Mexico has been that a group of central bureaucrats have "kidnapped" the decisions of families and irresponsibly misspent the national wealth (Olmedo Carranza, 1999, pp. 100-101).

I asked Dr. Raúl Olmedo Carranza, one of the foremost experts on Tlaxcala, whether the community governments are able to handle their new administrative responsibilities. Dr. Olmedo Carranza responded in the affirmative. He said that they are able to make the simple budgets, plans, reports, etc. that are required to carry out their development projects (R. Olmedo Carranza, personal communication, August 17, 2004).

The World Bank experience with the process of decentralization has caused it to recommend that people be allowed to learn by doing rather than requiring that fully developed expertise be acquired before decentralizing. "Decentralization in the absence of adequate local capacity was once considered undesirable, but that view is changing as experience shows that local capacities expand best as decentralized systems mature" (World Bank, 2003, p. 191). Indeed, the history of Tlaxcala showed that communities learned to play politics during the 1985-1995 period by serving as municipal agents.

On the other hand, the World Bank also recommends that "fostering capacity is best done in partnership between the center and subnational governments" (World Bank, 2003, p. 191). The challenge, once again, is to find the proper pace of decentralization. The history of Tlaxcala's decentralization illustrates an effective pace. Serving as municipal agents developed the essential skills required to establish relatively autonomous community governments. The policy recommendation would be to balance training by higher, more experienced levels of government with learning as you go

Equal Per Capita Distribution of Funds

As noted earlier, the state uses a very simple mechanism for distributing federal grants: 80% of the resources are distributed on an equal per capita basis; the other 20% is assigned according to the degree of community poverty. The formula has been simplified compared to the formula for distributing *FAIS* funds described in chapter 5 that takes into account several poverty indicators.

The use of formulas to distribute funds is desirable because they increase transparency and reduce the possibility of corruption and capture by elites. But why distribute 80% of the funds on an equal per capita basis? The disadvantage of an equal per capita distribution is that a community of 1,000 wealthy people receives the same amount of money as a community of 1,000 poor people. The money is not directed to where it is most needed.

One advantage of the approach is that it is comprehensible and transparent, thus reducing the risk of corruption. The state publishes the amount of *FAIS* funds received in its official bulletin. Each municipality, in turn, is required to let its citizens know the amount of money that it is receiving by posting announcements in public places. Municipalities and communities can easily verify that they have received the correct amount by multiplying the state grant per capita by the number of persons in the community.

The formulas of chapter 5 for distributing federal money are, in the abstract, more just. The trouble is that "nobody understands them," so communities are never sure that they received the correct amount of money (Olmedo Carranza, personal communication, August 18, 2004). Policymakers should assess the degree to which politics are pro-poor and honest, and they should use their assessment to balance the transparency of the equal per capita approach with the equity of more complex formulas.

Long-Term View

Mexico's structure of federal grants may have influenced the demand by citizens for the formation of municipalities that are small and not economically viable. The communities that made those demands may have been thinking more in terms of receiving a larger share of federal grants, than in terms of taxing themselves in order to pay for their own public goods and services. If taxing powers are eventually decentralized, these municipalities will find themselves in a difficult situation. It is good for policymakers to take a long-term view and to avoid establishing municipalities that will eventually become counter-productive.

Empirical Evidence

The decentralization model of chapters 2-3 strongly suggests that decentralizing through creating more units of government can be an effective approach to satisfying the basic needs of the poor. It can be especially powerful in strengthening the voice and client power of the voiceless, and in increasing the participation of the poor in the development process.

Still, there is a lack of empirical studies that *prove* the effectiveness of community governments in supplying public goods and services to the poor. An impact study by the Instituto Nacional de Administración Pública, A.C., of Mexico City is due to be published in 2005. Beyond this, the main empirical evidence is the multitudinous project reports of the communities (Olmedo Carranza, personal communication, July 22, 2003).

This chapter raises a host of empirical questions, including: What number of new governments is most effective in satisfying the basic needs of the poor? What should be their responsibilities? Which social infrastructure projects are community governments most capable of providing? What happens to the cost and quality of services as the number of government units per person changes? What are the administrative requirements and how can they best be met? What conditions are most propitious to increasing the number of government units and to defining their responsibilities? Developing empirically verified answers to these and other questions offers a fertile field for future research. Policymakers should be aware that the studies do not as yet exist.

CONCLUSION

Tlaxcala presents a new approach to implementing a basic needs approach to development: decentralize by increasing the number of governmental units. It can be fruitful. It can be done. The new units may be independent municipalities or dependent, semiautonomous community governments.

All of Latin America has been subject to conquest. It could be that the colonial origins of municipalities throughout the continent have caused them to be oversized and underrepresentative of the poor. If so, the policy recommendation is to consider following Tlaxcala's ground-breaking path of creating more units of government.

A study of the experiences of more than 60,000 poor people from 50 countries concluded that one of the most common complaints of the poor is a sense of hopelessness, powerlessness, humiliation and marginalization associated with a lack of voice and client power (Narayan et al., 2000, p. 39). Another is the maltreatment, corruption, and ineffectiveness of government services that come from the associated lack of accountability (Narayan et al., 1999, p. 98). Tlaxcala's unique form of decentralization may not be perfect, but in the end it may strike down two of the most persistent causes of poverty, the lack of voice and client power.

NOTES

1. The history of Tlaxcala's decentralization is derived from Olmedo Carranza, chapters 4-6
2. The description of delivering infrastructure to the poor is based on Olmedo Carranza, 1999, chapter 8.

CHAPTER 8

WORLD BANK TAX ADVICE

Does It Foster Inclusive Development?

The vertical equity of state intervention in Latin America could be seriously questioned

—Inter-American Development Bank

INTRODUCTION

The preceding chapters referred in large part to the decentralization of government expenditures to satisfy the basic needs that create a more inclusive development process. The other side of the coin is taxation. The nature of the tax system determines who pays the bill for the basic goods and services. If the poor pay the taxes that are used to satisfy basic needs, the government takes with one hand and gives with the other. This delays the implementation of an inclusive development process.

The first issue for taxation to satisfy basic needs is to determine who pays the tax bill. Another issue is the question of whether the taxes should be decentralized. We have seen the advantages of decentralizing expenditures (chapter 4). Do similar advantages exist for decentralizing taxes?

Decentralization for Satisfying Basic Needs: An Economic Guide for Policymakers, 2nd Edition
pp. 101–126

The World Bank (WB) exercises a strong influence on Latin American tax systems. It gives tax "advice," and it makes following the advice a condition for receiving development loans on preferential terms. Not surprisingly, all Latin American countries have followed the outlines of the WB tax advice.

Consequently, practitioners need to know the advice that this prestigious institution is offering and understand its impact on satisfying the basic needs that generate an inclusive development process. The purpose of this chapter is to describe and to explain the tax advice of the WB, and to analyze it in terms of its effects on satisfying the basic needs of the poor. Chapter 9 continues the theme of taxation by presenting a case study of a tax reform that follows the WB guidelines, that of El Salvador.

FISCAL MODEL

Chapter 1 showed that approximately one of every four persons in Latin America lives on less than $2 a day. At the same time, Latin America is the most unequal region of the world. This poverty and inequality bring domination, exploitation and exclusion of the poor from the development process.

In Chapter 2, we saw that the best solution for Latin America's poverty and inequality must include a development process that benefits all of the people, not just a small subset of society. In order to create an inclusive development process, it is necessary to satisfy basic needs such as health and education that increase the productivity of the poor. The higher productivity generates new opportunities for employment and for earning sufficient income to live a full life.

The decentralization model presented in Chapter 4 treated the question of which level of government should supply the basic goods and services that increase the productivity of the excluded. The best level of government is the level whose jurisdiction encompasses the beneficiaries of the good or service. The central government ought to supply the goods and services that benefit the entire nation. The states and municipalities should supply the goods and services that benefit the people of their respective jurisdictions. Given that the benefits of basic goods and services such as primary education and health care are generally confined to states and municipalities, these governments ought to assume primary responsibilities for supplying them.

The advantage of decentralizing the supply of basic goods and services to sub-national governments is that it helps these governments adapt to the specific needs of their jurisdictions. Frequently, the benefits of basic goods and services are confined to small regions, and needs vary between regions. Decentralization gives subnational governments the flexibility required to respond appropriately. At the same time, decentralization strengthens voice so that the people may better express their specific needs and monitor the supply of the goods and services.

Taxation plays a decisive role in generating an inclusive development process. First, taxation raises the funds necessary to pay the costs of satisfying basic needs. Second, *progressive* taxation speeds the process of generating an inclusive development process, while *regressive* taxation has the opposite effect. For example, taxing a low-income family that lives on the margin of existence in order to construct a new school tends to leave the family's children hungrier and less able to learn. The more effective approach is to tax the wealthy to pay the costs of the school and enroll well-nourished children.

Progressive taxation for satisfying the basic needs of the poor implies a redistribution of income from the rich to the poor. Latin America's extreme inequality and the importance of implementing a basic needs approach to development in a short period of time justify this redistribution of income. Given that the costs of satisfying the basic needs of the poor tends to be low (chapter 2), the redistribution may not have to be large.

The theory of fiscal federalism (chapter 4) argues that in general the central government should carry out the redistribution of income. If a municipality, for example, adopts a redistribution policy that is significantly more aggressive than the policies of surrounding communities, it creates incentives for the rich to move out of the municipality and for the poor to move in. As the rich leave, the municipality is less able to tax the rich, and as the poor move in, the needs increase. The two migrations tend to undermine the attempt to satisfy basic needs by means of progressive taxation. Given that it is much more difficult to move out of a nation than out of a municipality or state, it is the central government that should impose progressive taxes on the rich. In short, progressive taxation should be centralized.

What, then, is the optimal fiscal policy for satisfying the basic needs of the poor in Latin America? The ideal is to: (1) *centralize* a progressive system of taxation; and (2) *decentralize* the supply of basic goods and services to the poor by transferring the centralized tax revenues to the subnational governments so that they may pay their costs of supplying basic goods and services. We saw in chapter 5 that Mexico's fiscal structure conforms nicely to this model, although it has yet to take full advantage of its fiscal arrangement.

The purist might recommend that taxes be decentralized because centralization separates taxing from spending. The separation tends to cause inefficient quantities of public goods and services because public goods seem to be free, and so people demand too many of them.

The purist's recommendation overlooks the extreme poverty and inequality of Latin America and the dire need for a redistribution of income through both taxing and spending. Chapter 4 showed that redistribution is primarily the responsibility of the central government. It seems counterproductive to decentralize taxes when poverty and inequality deprive the poor of the capacity to pay for the public goods and services that they might demand from government.

This chapter focuses on the tax system recommended by the WB to developing countries. The main question is: Does the WB recommend centralized progressive taxation to developing countries? If not, why not, and is the WB argument valid? Chapter 9 continues to address these questions by exploring the effects on El Salvador of following the WB tax advice.

WORLD BANK TAX ADVICE

The Web page of the WB (World Bank, 2009) declares that its tax advice is described and explained in two publications: (1) *Lessons in Tax Reform* (World Bank, 1991), and (2) the first chapter of *Tax Reform in Developing Countries* (Thirsk, 1997). The following description of the WB tax policy is based principally on these sources.

Origins

In the decade of the 1980s, the WB began giving tax advice to developing countries and requiring that the advice be followed in order to receive development loans on preferential terms (World Bank, 1991, pp. 7-10). Between 1980 and 1989, the WB made 94 adjustment loans of $12.63 billion. More than 90% of these loans included conditions for tax policy (World Bank, 1991, p. 73). It is also possible that the WB sways the tax policy of Latin American countries through its influence—direct or indirect—on other organizations such as the United States Agency for International Development (USAID) and the Inter-American Development Bank (IDB).

How to Design a Tax System

In order to explain the WB tax policy, we need to review the process of constructing a tax system. Designing a tax system is essentially a two-step process: (1) determine the objectives of the tax system, and (2) select a set of taxes that achieves the objectives.

First Step: Determine the Objectives

The economic circumstances of a country often determine the primary objective of the tax system. For example, if budget deficits (in which government spending exceeds revenues) are a concern, a country may adopt the primary objective of reforming the tax system so that it generates more revenue.

One may also select secondary objectives for the tax system. The principal source of these objectives is a list of "Requirements for a Good Tax Structure" that was developed by professors Richard and Peggy Musgrave in their classic work on public finance (Musgrave & Musgrave, 1989, p. 216). In short, a good tax system: (1) increases tax revenues sufficiently; (2) distributes the tax burden fairly ("tax equity"); (3) minimizes interference with economic decisions ("tax efficiency"); (4) facilitates fiscal policy in order to achieve full employment without inflation; (5) permits fair administration; (6) is understandable by the taxpayers; and (7) minimizes the cost of administration and compliance. Economists try to satisfy all of these conditions at least insofar as they do not undermine the primary objective. The secondary objectives of the WB tax advice are treated in Appendix A.

Second Step: Select the Taxes

The second step in constructing a tax system is to select a set of taxes that achieves above all the primary objective, and also the secondary objectives to the extent that they do not undermine the primary objective.

The process of designing a tax system shows that there is no one system that is definitely the best package of taxes for a particular country. One may debate not only the objectives, but also the particular taxes adopted in order to achieve the objectives. "There is no unique prescription for the design of a single tax or a system of taxes, nor is there a single country in which all taxes are optimally designed" (World Bank, 1991, pp. 57-58).

The World Bank's Primary Objective

The WB followed the standard process of designing a tax system in order to develop its tax advice: first it studied the economic context in order to select its primary objective, and then it selected a set of taxes that seemed suitable for achieving the objective. The WB adopted other secondary objectives to the extent that they supported the primary objective. Appendix A treats the secondary objectives of the WB.

The Economic Context: The International Debt Crisis

In the early 1950s, Latin America began to adopt the approach to development called "import substitution industrialization" (ISI). One justification for the approach was dependency theory which argued that Latin America was underdeveloped because it was *dependent* upon the industrialized world. The solution was to become *independent*. How? By industrializing and producing at home the goods and services that were being imported.

In order to industrialize, Latin American governments began spending huge sums of money for investments in public enterprises, infrastructure, subsidies to private enterprise, and other items that were thought to contribute to industrialization. These expenditures generated large fiscal deficits. A sample of 33 developing countries showed that the public sector had an average fiscal deficit of 7% of gross domestic product (GDP) in 1986 (Chhibber & Khalilzadeh-Shirazi, 1988, cited in World Bank, 1991, p. 17). In comparison, the large fiscal deficit of the United States in 2008 was only 3.2% of its GDP (Congressional Budget Office, 2009).

If expenditures are larger than revenues, how can the governments pay their bills? One answer was to borrow money from the banks of the United States and other industrialized countries. Between 1973 and 1983, the international debt of Latin America increased from 23% to almost 47% of it GDP (Sachs & Larrain, 1993, Table 22-1, p. 691).

After an initial burst of industrialization, ISI wavered. Production and income hardly grew at all during the "lost decade" of the 1980s (Franco, 2003, Table 3.3, p. 65). Latin America failed to achieve the import substitution that it needed in order to pay its international debt. In 1982, Mexico defaulted on the payment of its debt, and other countries were in danger of following suit.

Suddenly, United States banks that had loaned many billions of dollars to Latin America—and the international banking system in general—were in danger of collapse. "In 1982, the exposure of nine top U.S. based banks to shaky foreign loans was twice the value of their own paid-in capital" (Lindert & Pugel, 1996, p. 570). International loans to Latin American governments skidded to a halt.

The situation was critical and something had to be done immediately. World Bank economists concluded that a key for resolving the crisis was to eliminate the fiscal deficits that were forcing governments to borrow, and to generate fiscal surpluses that would make it possible for them to pay their debts. One way to achieve this was to increase tax revenues.

Primary Objective: Tax Revenues

In this way the primary objective of the WB came to be that of increasing tax revenues as rapidly as possible. The WB declared:

> How to contain and rationalize an over-expanded public sector has become one of the principle challenges facing many developing countries in recent

> years. In this context, the rationale for tax reform is twofold: first ... reduce ... inefficiencies and inequities in the allocation of resources; and second, ... *generate public revenue*." (emphasis added) (World Bank, 1991, p. 2).

Here, the WB declares that its primary objective is to reduce inefficiencies and inequities, and that its secondary objective is to generate public revenue. However, the argument of this chapter is that in fact the primary objective of the tax advice is to generate revenues in order to resolve the debt crisis. Appendix A argues that the traditional concepts of tax efficiency and equity were reinterpreted and pursued only insofar as they contributed to the primary objective of increasing tax revenues.

World Bank Advice for Increasing Tax Revenues

The WB tax advice for increasing tax revenues contains two parts: (1) restructure the tax system, and (2) increase the number of tax payers. The WB offered many recommendations for accomplishing this. This section describes the recommendations that have the greatest impact on satisfying basic needs and on generating an inclusive development process.

Strategy I: Restructure the Tax System

The Value-Added Tax. In order to increase tax revenues, the WB recommends that countries introduce a new tax, the value-added tax (VAT), and that this tax be the main source of revenues: "Revenue would be generated primarily by a broadly based domestic tax on consumption.... The best instrument to achieve this objective would be a VAT" (World Bank, 1991, p. 57).

Revenue Generator. The VAT is a good revenue generator partly because it taxes a wide range of sales, and partly because it is easier to administer than the best alternative, the personal income tax:

> If developing countries are unable to make personal income taxes work effectively (because of tax evasion, accounting difficulties, long collection lags, and other enforcement problems), it may be the better part of wisdom to aim instead for the achievement of an efficient indirect tax system (Thirsk, 1997, p. 15).

It is relatively easy to administer the VAT partly because the tax contains a self-enforcing feature. The VAT is implemented by taxing the total value of all sales at all stages of production. It becomes a tax on the value-added at each stage of production by the government refunding the taxes that were paid in earlier stages of production. However, in order to get a refund, the producer must show a receipt for the taxes paid earlier. Consequently, each taxpayer insists that the taxes due at earlier stages of production were in fact paid, and that the receipts are transferred to the next buyer.

The Personal Income Tax. Normally, successive blocks of personal income are taxed at increasing marginal rates. For example, the first $10,000 of a person's income may be taxed at a marginal rate of 5%, and the second $10,000 at a marginal rate of 10% and so forth. The second recommendation of the WB for increasing revenue is to lower the maximum marginal tax rate of the Personal Income tax to 30-50% (World Bank, 1991, p. 43).

Revenue Generator. The purpose of reducing the maximum marginal tax rate on personal income is to increase revenues by reducing the incentive to evade the tax (World Bank, 1991, p. 43). The thinking is that if people gain less by evading the tax, they will evade less. If evasion drops more than the tax rate, revenues increase.

The recommendation to lower the maximum marginal rate on the Personal Income Tax is closely connected with the administrative reforms treated below. One aim of these reforms is to force more people from all income classes to pay their taxes.

The Tax on Business Profit. The recommendation for the tax on business profits is to establish one fixed rate approximately equal to the maximum marginal tax rate of the personal income tax (World Bank, 1991, p. 58).

Revenue Generator. The single rate on business profits makes it easier to administer and to pay the tax, and, at the same time, it makes evasion more difficult. The lower rate also reduces the incentive to utilize tax arbitrage in which businesses manipulate accounting procedures in order to hide the true sources of profits and thereby reduce taxes.

Strategy II: Increase the Number of Taxpayers

The second WB strategy for increasing revenues is to increase the number of taxpayers, or, in other words, to "broaden the tax base." The first way to broaden the tax base is to implement a wide range of administrative reforms. The reforms include simplifying the tax system in order to make it easier to administer. Other recommendations include additional training for administrators, attracting more qualified personnel by increasing salaries, computerizing, and reorganizing tax departments (World Bank, 1991, pp. 51-54).

The second way to broaden the tax base is to implement the VAT. We saw earlier that the self-enforcing feature of the VAT tends to reduce evasion. Another advantage of the VAT is that it has a broader base than the earlier taxes on international trade and internal production (World Bank, 1991, p. 31).

The third way to broaden the tax base is to institute legal reforms that close legal loopholes for avoiding taxes, and that stiffen sanctions for evasion. The fourth way is to reduce the number of exemptions from both the VAT and the Personal Income Tax (World Bank, 1991, pp. 31, 35). Finally, in order to assure timely payments, the WB recommends the extending the use of withholding systems for taxes such as the Personal Income Tax (World Bank, 1991, p. 58).

INCIDENCE

Tax incidence is the distribution of the tax burden among individuals. A tax may be regressive, proportional or progressive. A tax is progressive if the percentage of income paid as tax (tax/income) increases as personal income *increases*. The tax is regressive if the percentage increases as income *decreases*. The tax is proportional if the percentage paid is constant over different classes of income.

The Fiscal Model argues that centralized progressive taxation better serves the objective of implementing an inclusive development process through satisfying basic needs. The aim of this section is to examine the incidence of the WB tax recommendations.

Value-Added Tax

The WB recommends that the VAT be the principal source of tax revenues. Economic analysis concludes that the VAT is a regressive tax because consumers pay it (they cannot shift the tax to others), and because the poor spend a relatively large percentage of their incomes on consumption items (Musgrave & Musgrave, 1989, pp. 399, 404).

Table 8.1 illustrates the regressivity of the VAT. The table shows two individuals. The first earns $730 a year ($2 per day) while the other earns $100,000. The lower income person is forced by necessity to spend all of his income for goods and services that are subject to the VAT. The relatively rich person saves 30% of his income and spends $70,000 to buy goods and services taxed by the VAT.

Table 8.1. Regressivity of the Value Added Tax

(1)	(2)	(3)	(4)	(5)	(6)
Income	*Consumption*	*Savings*	*Rate (%)*	*Tax ($)*	*Tax/Income*
$730	$730	$0	10	$73	10%
$100,000	$70,000	$30,000	10	$7,000	7%

Column (5) shows that a VAT of 10% yields $73 of tax revenue that is paid by the relatively poor taxpayer. In column (6) we see that the $73 tax bill is 10% of the poor person's income. Since the rich person pays the VAT on only $70,000, his tax bill of $7,000 is only 7% of his income. The VAT is regressive because the low-income person pays a relatively large percentage of his income as tax (10% vs. 7%). The source of the regressivity is that the VAT applies to the entire income of the poor person, but only to 70% of the rich person's income.

Latin America has implemented the WB tax advice for the VAT. The tax has been introduced in all Latin American countries (Tanzi, 1996, p. 24; CEPAL, 2006, p. 192). In addition, most of the countries have increased the tax rate of their VAT between the time that they first implemented the tax and 1993 (Tanzi, 1996, Table 2.2, p. 25).

The preference for the VAT is reflected in a relatively large increase in the revenues yielded by the tax. Between 1978 and 1988, taxes on personal income in Latin America increased from 1.6 to 1.7% of GDP, an increase of 6.25%. However, the revenues yielded by the VAT increased from 1.9 to 2.7% of GDP, a 42% increase in share of GDP (Tanzi, 1996, Table 2.1, p. 21).

The Personal Income Tax

Economic analysis shows that the personal income tax is a progressive tax. It is progressive because it is paid by the income earner (it is not shifted to others), and because the marginal tax rates increase over successive blocks of income (Musgrave & Musgrave, 1989, p. 256).

The WB recommends that the maximum marginal rate of the tax be lowered to 30-50%. This policy is regressive in the sense that it makes the tax less progressive than before.

Again, Latin America has implemented the WB tax advice. Between 1979 and 1991, the average of the maximum marginal tax rates of the personal income tax fell from 48.1% to 35.4% in a sample of 18 Latin American countries (Tanzi, 1996, Table 2.3, p. 26).

Tax on Business Profits

Economic analysis concludes that business owners pay the tax on business profits if they are trying to maximize profits (Musgrave & Musgrave, 1989, p. 265). If a business was maximizing profits before the tax, it cannot increase its profits by raising the price and thereby selling less than the profit maximizing quantity. It is better to be left with 75% of $1,000,000 than 75% of less than $1,000,000. This conclusion holds under both competitive and monopolistic conditions.

The tax on business profits is progressive insofar as the owners who receive the profits are relatively rich. The WB recommendation is to reduce the maximum marginal tax rate on business profits to that of the personal income tax. The recommendation is regressive in the sense that diminishing the maximum marginal rate makes the tax less progressive. In Latin America, the average tax rate on business profits fell from 43.5% to 36.3% of taxable profit between 1980 and 1991 (Tanzi, 1996, Table 2.4, p. 27).

Impact of Regressive Taxes on the Development Process

The WB recommendations for tax reform include highly regressive elements: it makes the regressive VAT sales tax the main source of revenue, and it lowers the progressivity of the income taxes. As a result, the poor are left with less disposable income for purchasing food and other basic goods and services in the private market place. This slows the satisfaction of basic needs that enhance productivity and the implementation of an inclusive development process.

A CRITICAL ASSUMPTION

There is no doubt that the WB is fully aware that regressive taxes obstruct the satisfaction of basic needs. Nevertheless, the WB argues that given the extreme inequality of Latin America, following its tax advice is the most effective approach.

According to the WB, history teaches that it is impossible to impose a progressive tax structure in Latin America. Many attempts have been made to impose progressive taxes, and they have failed. Occasionally, progressive taxes have been legislated, but it has been impossible to enforce the law. Hence, the WB makes a crucial leap: It assumes that the "second best" policy is to abandon the attempt, and to focus on using tax revenues to satisfy basic needs. Thirsk writes:

> There seems to be increasing acceptance of the notion that the tax system as a whole may be an extremely poor vehicle for redistributing income. In none of the countries studied has a pre-reform schedule of progressive tax rates successfully generated a progressive distribution of tax burdens. If developing countries are unable to make personal income taxes work effectively (because of tax evasion, accounting difficulties, long collection lags, and other enforcement problems), it may be the better part of wisdom to aim instead for the achievement of an efficient indirect tax system and use its revenues to finance targeted subsidies for the poor. Ultimately, it is fiscal rather than tax incidence that affects people's welfare. (Thirsk, 1997, p. 15)

Perhaps the biggest obstacle to progressive taxation cited in this statement is "other enforcement problems." One "other enforcement problem" is that the extreme economic inequality creates a concentration of political power, and, with it, the capacity to obstruct attempts to implement a progressive tax system.

That it is impossible to use progressive taxes in Latin America is a key assumption of the WB with possibly devastating consequences. The danger is that the resulting WB strategy permanently locks into place the inequality that is at the root of Latin America's failure to satisfy basic needs and generate an inclusive development process.

Is the assumption valid? What would have happened to the Blacks of the United States if Dr. Martin Luther King had abandoned the long and difficult journey of combating the traditional racism of the Whites? Did Barak Obama become President of the United States by assuming that it is impossible for a Black man to win the presidential election? What would have happened to economic progress if thousands of inventors had abandoned their searches because what they were attempting had never been done before? The WB's impossibility assumption is surely a weak link in the development of its strategy.

TAX EVASION

Tax evasion reduces the revenues needed to satisfy basic needs. Evasion by the wealthiest class is especially important, not only because it lowers revenues, but also because it deepens the inequality and political control that can obstruct progressive taxation, the satisfaction of basic needs, and the implementation of an inclusive development process.

The WB assumes that making the income taxes less progressive will reduce tax evasion because the evasion is made less rewarding. The purpose of this section is to argue that after the reform, ample economic incentives to evade taxes remain. Economic incentives, together with the political power to evade taxes that is granted by extreme inequality, makes it unlikely that evasion by the ruling class will be diminished by making the income taxes less progressive.

Table 8.2 presents a simple case that is divided into two parts. The upper part (rows 1-9) treats the period before the tax reform. The lower part (rows 10-18) treats the period after the reform. The first row of the table shows the taxable incomes of two individuals, one poor and the other a millionaire. The poor person earns $2 a day, or $730 a year, and pays no income tax. He pays the sales tax of 8%.

It is assumed that, before the tax reform, the effective tax rate on the income of the millionaire (the percentage of total income that is paid as a tax) is 40%, and that he also pays the sales tax of 8%. After the reform, the

Table 8.2. Incentives for Tax Evasion

Prereform: Effective Rate on Income = 40%, VAT = 8%			
	Poor	*Evasion = 0%*	*Evasion = 100%*
1. Taxable income	$730	$1,000,000	$1,000,000
2. Personal income tax	$0	$400,000	$0
3. Net income (1-2)	$730	$600,000	$1,000,000
4. Consumption (50% of net income	$730	$300,000	$500,000
5. VAT	$58.40	$24,000	$0
6. Savings (50% of net income)	$0	$300,000	$500,000
7. Interest (6%)	$0	$18,000	$30,000
8. Net income (1-2-5+7)	$671.60	$594,000	$1,030,000
9. Inequality ratio			1,534
Postreform: Effective Rate on Income = 25%; VAT = 13%			
	Poor	*Evasion = 0%*	*Evasion = 100%*
10. Taxable income	$730	$1,000,000	$1,000,000
11. Personal income tax	$0	$250,000	$0
12. Net income (10-11)	$730	$750,000	$1,000,000
13. Consumption	$730	$375,000	$500,000
14. VAT	$94.90	$48,750	$0
15. Savings	$0	$375,000	$500,000
16. Interest (6%)	$0	$22,500	$30,000
17. Net income (10-11-14+16)	$635.10	$723,750	$1,030,000
18. Inequality ratio		1,140	1,622

effective rate of the income tax falls to 25%, and the VAT is implemented at a rate of 13%. In chapter 9 we will see that these figures correspond to the experience of El Salvador.

Row 8 shows that if the millionaire evades all of his taxes before the reform, and if he earns 6% interest on his savings of $500,000, he is left with a net income of $1,030,000 at the end of the year.

Row 17 shows that if the reform eliminates the evasion, the millionaire's net income falls to $723,750. However, if he continues evading his taxes after the reform his income remains at $1,030,000. Consequently, evading during the postreform period increases the income of the wealthy person by $306,250, no less than 42%. Evading half of his taxes leaves him with an additional $153,125, a gain of 21%. Clearly, the millionaire has a strong economic incentive to continue evading his taxes.

Rows 9 and 18 show "inequality ratios," the net income of the rich divided by that of the poor. Row 9 shows that if, before the tax reform, the millionaire evades 100% of his taxes, his income is 1,534 times that of the poor person. Row 18 shows that if the evasion is eliminated in the postreform period, the inequality ratio falls by 35% to 1,140. The millionaire loses substantial economic and social superiority, and this diminishes his political influence.

On the other hand, if the millionaire continues evading his taxes after the reform, the inequality ratio rises from 1,534 to 1,622. The millionaire not only preserves his economic power, but also increases it. Further calculations would show that the increase grows very significantly over time. The source of the increase of the ratio in the table is the increase in VAT payments by the poor.

Clearly, strong economic incentives exist for wealthy persons to continue evading their taxes after the reform. Not evading puts the traditional economic, social and political order at risk. Why not use the extreme inequality and the resulting political control to continue evading taxes and thereby strengthen the established order?

WORLD BANK STRATEGY

After assuming that it is impossible to impose progressive taxes in Latin America, the WB strategy becomes one of raising revenues through making the tax structure more regressive, broadening the tax base, and focusing on spending to satisfy basic needs. Are revenues likely to be increased? And are additional revenues likely to be spent to satisfy the basic needs of the poor?

Table 8.3. Reform, Evasion and Tax Revenues

	Prereform: Effective Tax on Income = 40%; Sales = 8%		
	Poor	*Evasion = 0%*	*Evasion = 100%*
1. Taxable income	$730	$1,000,000	$1,000,000
2. Income tax revenue	$0	$400,000	$0
3. VAT	$58.40	$24,000	$0
4. Tax revenue	$58.40	$424,000	$0
5. Total tax revenue		$424,058.40	$58.40
	Postreform: Effective Tax on Income = 25%; VAT = 13%		
	Poor	*Evasion = 0%*	*Evasion = 100%*
7. Taxable income	$730	$1,000,000	$1,000,000
8. Income tax revenue	$0	$250,000	$0
9. VAT	$94.90	$48,750	$0
10. Tax revenue	$94.90	$298,750	$0
11. Total tax revenue		$298,844.90	$94.90

More Tax Revenues?

Table 8.3 continues the case of Table 8.2 in order to give an idea of the impact of the tax reform on the tax revenues received by the government. The tax revenues are simply the sums of the taxes paid in Table 8.2.

If we compare row 5 to row 11, we see that eliminating evasion by the wealthy increases total tax revenues from $58.40 before the reform to $298,844.90 after the reform. Obviously, eliminating tax evasion by the millionaire generates a large increase in tax revenues.

The more probable case is that the evasion continues after the reform because of the strong economic incentives and political power to do so. In this case, total tax revenues increase only slightly from $58.40 to $94.90. The increase comes from payment by the poor of the VAT at a higher tax rate.

This is not to say that the reform will not generate a significant increase in tax revenues. Revenues may be increased by increasing the number of taxpayers. If the wealthiest evade their taxes, the additional revenues come from the low and middle income classes. This increases the concentration of income in the highest income class.

More Spending?

The strategy of the WB is to increase tax revenues by more regressive taxation and then focus on spending part of the increase to satisfy basic needs. A very important question arises immediately in the Latin American context of extreme inequality: If it is impossible to impose progressive taxes on the wealthy to satisfy basic needs, then how can they be forced to spend tax revenues to satisfy basic needs? The question is especially pertinent if the tax reform exacerbates the inequality in the highest income bracket. Do the wealthy have a good will with respect to expenditures that they do not have with respect to taxes? Will they not prefer to spend mainly in ways that directly serve their own short-term interests?

Empirical data suggest that the WB tax reform has done little to increase government spending for basic goods and services. A review of the Latin American tax reforms conducted by Inter-American Development Bank (IDB) found that, despite the "urgent necessity" to increase spending to satisfy basic needs, the spending has not taken place:

> Recent reforms sought to improve tax collection by increasing the neutrality of the tax system, complemented by a reform in government spending to meet the needs of the poorest groups more efficiently. Nevertheless, spending reforms have lagged, and in fact the vertical equity of state intervention in Latin America could be seriously questioned (Rey de Marulanda, 1996, p. 7).

Similarly, the WB found that "between the mid-1980s and mid-1990s public spending on education and health increased in a large number of low-income countries, though slowly" (World Bank, 2001, p. 82). In addition, the education and health spending that took place frequently benefited the rich more than the poor (World Bank 2001, p. 80). In 1993, for example, only 9% of the Nicaraguan budget for education benefited the poorest segment of the population, while 40% of the budget benefited the richest segment (World Bank 2001, Table 5.1, p. 80).

CONCLUSION

In order to solve the financial crisis caused by the international debt crisis, the WB made the primary objective of its tax advice that of increasing revenues as quickly and easily as possible. The problem was to find the tax system that would achieve the objective in the Latin American context of extreme poverty and inequality.

Progressive taxes are clearly preferable in the context of extreme poverty and inequality. However, the WB based its tax advice on the critical assumption that it is impossible to impose progressive taxes in Latin America. Hence, the strategy became one of ignoring tax equity, focusing only on raising tax revenues, and hoping that additional spending for basic goods and services will follow. Revenues are to be increased by imposing more regressive taxes and by increasing the number of taxpayers.

Regressive taxation slows the satisfaction of the basic needs that enhance the productivity of the poor and generate an inclusive development process. It takes money out of the pockets of the poor that could have been used to purchase basic goods and services in the market place. It sends hungry children to new school buildings.

The incidence of the WB tax reform depends partly on evasion. The wealthiest and most powerful people in Latin America have the economic incentive and probably the political power to evade their taxes even in the face of WB reform. This tax evasion can solidify a class structure that obstructs progressive taxation and the satisfaction of basic needs.

Without intending to do so, the WB tax advice may have deepened and perpetuated an extreme inequality that obstructs the satisfaction of basic needs and the generation of an inclusive development process. Short-term gains in revenue and small increases in expenditures for basic needs may have been exchanged for long-term condemnation to the status quo, to poverty and inequality.

Policymakers should reevaluate the critical assumption that it is impossible to implement progressive tax systems in Latin America. Is it not possible that political developments in Latin America coupled with support from international institutions and developed countries could implement progressive taxation? If so, the WB has made a false assumption with potentially disastrous long-term consequences. The timely implementation of an inclusive development process requires progressive taxation. The extreme inequality and poverty that afflict Latin America further justify progressive taxation. How can the endeavor be abandoned?

Latin America would be well-served by changing the primary objective of its tax systems from raising tax revenues as easily as possible to instituting an inclusive development process. In order to achieve this objective in a timely manner, taxes should be made more progressive. Policymakers should begin by attacking the tax evasion, especially that of the wealthiest persons. Next, they should make tax systems more progressive. The most obvious way to do this is to raise the maximum marginal rates on the income taxes and to lower the VAT rates. Chapter 9 cites the importance of national taxes on property, gifts, and inheritances.

The WB has recommended some constructive administrative reforms such as the elimination of politically motivated and inefficient tax exemptions. Policymakers should adopt the reforms that serve of objective of implementing an inclusive development process.

As more progressive taxation raises revenues, policymakers should increase expenditures to satisfy the basic needs of the poor. This requires implementing the effective service delivery model proposed in chapters 3 and 4.

The WB is correct in asserting that history teaches that implementing progressive taxation in Latin America is a formidable challenge. There is no doubt that Latin American politicians operate in difficult circumstances. They must fight centuries of traditions in which governments have been more concerned with serving the powerful rather than serving the common good. Success depends on their receiving much support. The primary and most important source of that support must be the political participation of the citizen/clients who elect the politicians and to whom they express their voice and client power. Another important source of support must be international institutions like the WB. Chapter 10 analyzes the way that developed nations might tailor their foreign aid to foster inclusive development.

APPENDIX A: SECONDARY OBJECTIVES

We have seen that the primary objective of the WB tax advice is to increase revenues rapidly in order to alleviate the international debt crisis. The WB also adopted secondary objectives from the list of requirements for a good tax Structure. This section treats two important examples, tax equity and tax efficiency. The argument here is that the WB designed its tax policy in order to maximize revenues, and afterwards it sought equity and efficiency in the policy that it had already designed. In doing this, the WB redefined and limited the traditional meaning of the terms, and it gave an exaggerated impression of the equity and efficiency of its tax advice.

Equity

Economists define two types of tax equity. The first, named horizontal equity means that everybody in the same income class pays the same amount of tax. The second, vertical equity, means that there is a fair distribution of the tax burden across different income classes. A fair tax system is characterized by both horizontal and vertical equity.

Horizontal Equity in the Tax Advice

Lowering the maximum marginal tax rates on income supposedly reduces tax evasion and thereby helps to assure that everybody in the same income class pays the same amount of tax. Administrative reforms that improve enforcement of the tax laws tend to have the same effect.

Similarly, tax withholding can stimulate timely tax payments and reduce evasion. Eliminating exemptions from the income tax—especially if they were politically motivated—also helps to improve horizontal equity. The prescriptions of the WB for increasing revenue clearly provide a bonus of improving horizontal equity.

Vertical Equity in the Tax Advice

What about Vertical Equity? Although the VAT is a good source of revenue, it also happens to be a regressive tax. Both instituting the VAT and increasing its tax rate increase the regressivity of the tax system. Furthermore, lowering the maximum marginal rates of the income taxes diminishes the progressivity of those taxes. These are two important ways in which the WB tax advice violates the principle of vertical equity. It increases the tax that burdens the poor relatively heavily, and it diminishes the tax bill of the wealthy.

Vertical equity is important in the Latin American context of extreme poverty and inequality that create a great need for inclusive development. Recognizing this, the WB tries to salvage some vertical equity by making adjustments to the VAT and the personal income tax.

In the case of the VAT, the WB recommends that products that are consumed by the poor, such as unprocessed food, be exempted from it. It also recommends that relatively high tax rates be imposed on the sale of luxury items that are consumed mainly by the well-to-do (World Bank, 1991, p. 6).

However, there is disagreement within the WB about these attempts to alleviate the regressivity of the VAT. Thirsk argues, perhaps realistically, that governments should not try to alleviate the regressivity of the VAT in this way "because it complicates the administration of the VAT and is an example of poor targeting between tax instruments and objectives" (Thirsk, 1997, p. 21).

Another way proposed to salvage some vertical equity is to make an adjustment in the personal income tax. The WB recommends that persons of very low income be exempted from the payment of this tax (World Bank, 1991, pp. 60, 72).

Ineffective Exemptions

The WB itself declares that the policy of exempting items consumed by the poor from the VAT has not functioned well in practice: "None of the reforms examined appear to have achieved notable success in reducing indirect tax burdens on the poor, although, ... most countries try to remove some of the VAT burden on the poor by exempting unprocessed food products" (Thirsk, 1997, p. 24).

The recommendation to exempt persons of very low income from the Personal Income Tax probably has very little effect on vertical equity because most income taxes are paid by government employees and workers of large firms, most of whom are not poor (World Bank, 1991, p. 16). The poorest people work in the informal sector and do not pay the income tax.

More Adequate Definition of Equity

There is a temptation to interpret horizontal and vertical equity solely in vague terms of justice. It is "fair" that everyone of the same income class pay the same tax, and it is "fair" to have an equitable distribution of taxes among persons of distinct income classes. The problem with this interpretation is that "fairness" is an abstract and vague concept that has never received widespread acceptance as a political objective.

In the context of Latin America, the traditional interpretation of equity should be broadened and concretized so that it includes inclusive development. Much of the practical importance of horizontal and vertical equity is that it gives the poor majority the opportunity to attain a better life through full participation in the production process. Inequity robs them of this opportunity.

Conclusion

The WB tax policy worsens the vertical inequity of the Latin American tax systems. It is an unjust policy for the Latin American context of extreme inequality and poverty. However, its most serious failure may be that maintaining or increasing the tax burdens of the poor delays the implementation of an inclusive development process by taking money out of their pockets and reducing their ability to purchase the basic goods and services that they need to increase their productivity. The focus of the WB on horizontal equity, and its weak attempts to reduce its negative impact on vertical equity, give an exaggerated impression of the equity of its recommendations. A subtitle that is repeated in its publication is fallacious: "Tax reform can lower the burden on the poor" (World Bank, 1991, pp. 6, 60).

EFFICIENCY

Meaning

Another secondary objective adopted by the WB is tax efficiency. Just as in the case of tax equity, the procedure of the WB is to search for efficiency in the recommendations that have already been established in order to increase revenues. Once again, the procedure leads the WB to redefine and diminish the full significance of the term.

The need for tax efficiency stems from the fact that taxes impose two types of burden on taxpayers. The first type of burden is the quantity of money paid by the taxpayer. The second type is called "excess burden." This is the cost of taxation over and above the financial payment by the taxpayer. This additional cost comes from the taxpayer changing his behavior because of the tax. For example, if a tax on the sale of medicine causes the poor to not buy medicine, an excess burden is created. It includes the suffering associated with prolonged sickness.

Economists have developed a theory of optimal taxation in order to identify the tax systems that minimize excess burden. Some have concluded that an efficient tax system is progressive: "The optimal tax system is progressive" (Rosen, 2005, pp. 340-343). "An interesting and important feature of optimal tax reforms is that they almost never endorse a uniform pattern of tax rates for either direct or indirect taxes" (Thirsk, 1997, p. 8).

From Uniform Taxes to Efficiency

Despite the fact that optimal tax theory concludes that uniform taxes are not efficient, the WB recommends more uniform tax rates in the name of efficiency. The means of making the rates more uniform include the reductions in the maximum marginal tax rates of the income taxes and the introduction of the VAT with its broad base. How did the WB arrive at the conclusion that more uniform rates make the tax system more efficient when optimal tax theory teaches that progressive taxes (with their differentiated rates) are efficient?

The first step is to argue that it is not practical to implement the prescriptions of optimal tax theory because of a lack of information, administrative capacity and political requirements (Thirsk, 1997, p. 10). We will see below that this argument is disputed.

The second step is to argue that country experience teaches that rather than trying to achieve optimal taxation, it is better to *improve* the efficiency by making tax rates more uniform: "All of the country studies adopt the rule of thumb that the cause of economic efficiency is best served by a less differentiated pattern of effective income tax rates" (Thirsk, 1997, p. 10).

Why? Because some differences are caused by "cascade taxes" that fall on the total value of the sale at each stage of production. These taxes arbitrarily distort relative prices and consumer decisions because a product that has five stages of production is taxed five times, and a product that has two stages of production is taxed only twice.

Also, some tax exemptions that were intended to stimulate investment in industrial projects were ineffective. Others were the result of corruption. "Most of the observed non-uniformity prior to reform has been found to be non-optimal and highly distorting" (Thirsk, 1997, p.10).

The third step is to diminish the concept of tax efficiency until it means nothing more than the elimination of "non-optimal and highly distorting" differentiations in tax rates. In the end, instead of the progressive taxes dictated by optimal tax theory, the "efficiency" of the WB only eliminates the differences in rates that distort consumer decisions. Suddenly, the WB tax advice appears not only "equitable," but also "efficient."

The Correct Policy for Achieving Efficiency

Clearly, eliminating tax differences that are "highly distorting" improves tax efficiency. Nevertheless, efficiency can be improved still more by instituting the differences dictated by Optimal Tax Theory. The correct policy is to eliminate inefficient tax differences *and to institute the efficient differences.*

Feasibility of Optimal Taxes

The WB discards some progressive taxes recommended by Optimal Tax Theory on the grounds that they are impractical due to an inability to satisfy information, administrative and political requirements. However, Newbery and Stern (1987) found that the necessary data are in fact available, and that they can be used to determine optimal tax reform (cited in Thirsk, 1997, p. 9). If they are correct, the information and administrative requirements of optimal taxation are not prohibitive.

Broader Definition of Efficiency

The normal interpretation of excess burden ought to explicitly take into account the inefficiency of excluding the majoring of the population from full participation in the production process through regressive taxation. This exclusion may well be the "change of behavior" that has the most negative impact on social welfare. Uniform tax rates are inefficient not simply because they fail to take into account the dictates of optimal tax theory, but also because they lead to a regressive tax system that obstructs the satisfaction of basic needs and the implementation of an inclusive development process.

APPENDIX B[1]: EMPIRICAL EVIDENCE—PROGRESSIVE TAXATION, BASIC NEEDS AND DEVELOPMENT

This book has argued that the most effective way to generate an inclusive development process is to satisfy the basic needs of the poor using centralized progressive taxation to raise the necessary revenues. The purpose of this appendix is to conduct an exploratory empirical analysis of the effect of satisfying basic needs and progressive taxation on the level of production.

The Model

The following equation defines the model to be tested:

$$GDPPC = g(DIR/TOT, LIEX)$$

Where:

$GDPPC$ = real gross domestic product per capita
DIR/TOT = (direct tax revenue)/(total tax revenue)
$LIEX$ = life expectancy at birth

GDPPC is the value of production by all resident producers in the economy at constant prices divided by the midyear population (United Nations, 2004, p. 270). Using per capita GDP eliminates the effect of population increases on production. Using constant prices eliminates the effect of price changes.

LIEX is the number of years a newborn infant would live if prevailing patterns of age-specific mortality rates at the time of birth were to stay the same throughout the child's life (United Nations, 2004, p. 272). Statistical studies show that LIEX is probably the best single number proxy for the satisfaction of basic needs (Streeten, Burki, Haq, Hicks, & Stewart, 1981, chapter 3). If people are more nourished, better educated and have other basic needs satisfied, they tend to live longer.

Economic theory shows that direct taxes are generally progressive (McGuire, 1990). Consequently, the variable *DIR/TOT*, total direct tax revenue divided by total tax revenue, is a measure—albeit an imperfect measure—of the progressivity of the tax system.

The equation measures the effect of satisfying basic needs (*LIEX*) and progressive taxation (*DIR/TOT*) on production (*GDPPC*). The hypothesis is that satisfying basic needs increases production by increasing the productivity of the poor. Progressive taxation increases production by providing government revenues that can be used to supply public goods and services to the poor. It also increases production by leaving more money in the pockets of the poor that can be used to purchase basic goods and services such as food and medicine that enhance their productivity. If the hypothesis is correct, the analysis should yield positive and significant coefficients for the two variables in the model.

Data were collected for 14 Latin American countries for the years, 1980, 1985, 1990, 1995, 2000 and 2005 (IMF, United Nations, various issues). The countries are Argentina, Bolivia, Chile, Colombia, Costa Rica, El Salvador, Guatemala, Mexico, Nicaragua, Panama, Paraguay, Peru, Uruguay and Venezuela. The sample includes almost all Central and South American countries. Brazil and Ecuador were omitted because of a lack of data.

A Fixed Effects Regression technique was used to estimate the relationship between progressive taxation, satisfying basic needs and the level of production. Fixed Effects Regression is the standard technique for analyzing data that consists of a variety of subjects (countries) over a range of time periods (1980-2005). The technique gives relatively reliable results by controlling for omitted and unmeasured variables that differ between cases (countries) but are constant over time.

Results

Column (2) of Table 8.4 shows the effect in isolation of satisfying basic needs on real per capita GDP. The coefficient of life expectancy (*LIEX*) is positive and highly significant at the 1% level of confidence. The F score indicates that the model is highly significant at the 1% level of confidence. Overall, life expectancy explains 45% of the variation in real GDP per capita.

Column (3) shows the effect in isolation of progressive taxation on real per capita GDP. The coefficient of *DIR/TOT* is positive and significant at the 5% level. The *F* score indicates that the model is highly significant at the 1% level. Overall, the progressivity of taxes explains 9% of the variation in real gross domestic product per capita.

Column (4) combines the two independent variables into one equation. *LIEX* and *DIR/TOT* remain significant at the 1% and 5% levels, respectively. The signs of the two variables remain positive. The *F* score indicates that the model remains highly significant at the 1% level. Overall,

Table 8.4 Basic Needs, Progressive Taxation and Development

Dependent Variable: Real GDP per Capita

(1)	*(2)*	*(3)*	*(4)*
Independent Variables	*Model #1*	*Model #2*	*Model #3*
Constant	−10,010.7 (−4.23)	1,443.1 (2.67)	−10,605.6 (−4.56)
LIEX	184.9 (5.32)*		179.6 (5.28)*
DIR/TOT		38.7 (2.15)**	32.8 (2.14)**
n	84	84	84
R^2 within	0.29	0.06	0.34
R^2 between	0.53	0.10	0.52
R^2 overall	0.45	0.09	0.46
Prob > *F*	0.0000	0.0000	0.0000

Note: *Significant at 1% level. **Significant at 5% level.

the two variables explain 46% of the variation in real gross domestic product per capita.

The results are consistent with the hypothesis that satisfying basic needs through progressive taxation enhances production and development. They are also consistent with the hypothesis that satisfying basic needs is a development program as well as a welfare program.

The results call into question the World Bank's policy of recommending regressive taxation to developing countries. If the coefficient of Model 3 is correct, for every 1% that the World Bank lowers the progressivity of taxes, it lowers per capita production by $33. The results suggest that the World Bank should revise its tax advice to emphasize direct taxes such as the income taxes, the national property tax, and the inheritance and gift taxes.

The results suggest that the World Bank's policy of encouraging expenditures for satisfying basic needs is correct. The coefficient of *LIEX* indicates that if an additional satisfaction of basic needs increases life expectancy by 1 year, real GDP per Capita rises by $180.

The results support the hypothesis that satisfying basic needs through progressive taxation enhances development, but they do not give definitive proof of the hypothesis.

To illustrate, regressions report relationships, but not causality. Consequently, causality could be in the other direction: a high GDPPC could be causing a high *LIEX* and *DIR/TOT*.

NOTE

1. Appendix B is coauthored by Drs. J. M. McGuire, N. Zanca, D. Mitchell, and L. Romay.

CHAPTER 9

TAX REFORM IN EL SALVADOR

Future tax reforms should focus on promoting equity.

—Claudino Pito, Inter-American Development Bank

INTRODUCTION

Chapter 8 analyzed the tax advice of the World Bank (WB) in terms of its influence on generating a process of inclusive development. In 1989, El Salvador embarked on a long-term tax reform that follows the guidelines set out by the WB. The purpose of this chapter is to present a case study that searches for insight into the effects of following the WB tax advice on satisfying the basic needs of the poor and creating an inclusive development process.

TAX REFORM

El Salvador's Tax System

Table 9.1 describes the taxes that existed in El Salvador when the reform began in 1989. Column (1) lists the names of the taxes, and column (2) describes the base on which each tax fell. The table divides the taxes into two categories, direct and indirect taxes.

Decentralization for Satisfying Basic Needs: An Economic Guide for Policymakers, 2nd Edition
pp. 127–140

Table 9.1. Tax Structure of El Salvador

(1) Tax	*(2)* Base
Direct Taxes	
Personal income	Personal income of both Salvadoran citizens and foreigners working in the country
Business income	Income of both national firms and foreign firms located in the country
Personal property	Property located within the nation that is owned by either Salvadoran citizens or foreigners
Business property	Property located within the nation that is owned by either Salvadoran or foreign business.
Transfers of property	
By sale	Transfers between persons of the ownership of real estate
By gift	Gifts and trusts
By inheritance	Transfer of ownership by inheritance and bequest
Indirect Taxes	
Imports	Imported merchandise
Exports	Exported merchandise
Excise sales	Purchase of select items such as alcohol and tobacco products
Use of services	Air and sea passage, vehicle registration, etc.
Productive and commercial activities	Licenses and permissions for production and commercial activities
Papel sellado	Acts, contracts and duties validated by means of the seal, "papel sellado"
Cascade	All sales, both intermediate and final

Source: Ministerio de Hacienda de El Salvador (1987, pp. 1-25).

Direct Taxes

Direct taxes are taxes "that fall immediately on persons" in the sense that persons are taxed directly, and they cannot shift the tax to someone else (Ministerio de Hacienda de El Salvador, Glosario). The personal income tax, for example, is a direct tax that is paid by the earner. Direct taxes include the income taxes on persons and businesses, national property taxes on persons and businesses, and the taxes on the transfers of property by means of sale, inheritances or gifts.

Indirect Taxes

Indirect taxes are taxes "imposed on specific consumer goods and services" (Ministerio de Hacienda de El Salvador, Glosario). Indirect taxes can be shifted to others. For example, vendors can shift general sales taxes to consumers by raising the prices of their goods and services.

The cascade tax falls on the total value of all sales of all goods and services, both intermediate and final. The value-added tax (VAT) is also a tax on all sales, both final and intermediate, but the base of this tax is limited to the value-added at each stage of production. The VAT is equivalent to a general tax on the sales of only final goods and services because the sum of the value-added at each stage of production equals the value of the final sale. The bases of the other taxes are self-explanatory.

Changes

Tax Structure

Table 9.2 lists the principle changes in El Salvador's tax structure since 1989. The table shows very significant reductions in the rates of direct taxes. The maximum marginal rate of the personal income tax has been reduced from 60% to 30%, and the total tax bill is limited to 25% of one's income. The national property tax, the tax on gifts and the tax on inheritances have all been eliminated.

As the rates of direct taxes have diminished, the rates on indirect taxes have increased. The most important changes are that the VAT has been substituted for the cascade tax, and the rate of the VAT has increased from 8% to 13%. In addition, exemptions from the VAT of basic food items consumed by the poor—beans, white corn, rice, unprocessed fruits and vegetables, milk and medicines—have been eliminated. The government introduced the special contribution, FOVIAL, which is a $0.20 per gallon tax on gasoline; the revenues from this tax are used for road construction and maintenance. Other special contributions have been introduced that are sales taxes on items such as sugar, tobacco, and alcohol. These taxes are currently yielding a small amount of revenue.

Other changes in indirect taxes have included the elimination of the tax on exports and the reduction of the maximum marginal rate on imports. The aim of these changes is to foster international trade. The taxes on services and the Papel Sellado have been eliminated because they yielded little revenue. The aim was to simplify the system and so free administrators to dedicate themselves to collecting other taxes of greater yield.

Table 9.2. Principle Changes in El Salvador's Tax Structure, 1990-2008

(1)	*(2)*
Tax	*Change*
Direct Taxes	
Income	
Personal income	Exemption from $1,750 to $2,630 Number of brackets from 24 to 7 Maximum marginal rate from 60% to 30% Maximum Effective Tax Rate to 25%
Business income	One rate of 25%
Property	
Personal property	Eliminated
Business property	Eliminated
Transfers of property	
By sale	
By gift	Eliminated
By inheritance	Eliminated
Indirect Taxes	
Imports	From 25 rates to 7 Maximum rate from 290% to 20% Rate on capital imports from 5% to 1%
Exports	Eliminated
Excise sales	
Use of services	Eliminated
Productive and commercial activities	Eliminated
Papel sellado	Eliminated
Cascade	Eliminated
VAT	Introduced to replace Cascade Rate from 8% to 13%. Exemptions on beans, white corn, rice, unprocessed fruits and vegetables, milk and medicines eliminated.
Special contribution (FOVIAL)	Introduced $0.20 per gallon of gasoline
Other	Introduced Special Contributions on the sale of sugar, etc.

Sources: Trigueros (n.d.); Ministerio de Hacienda de El Salvador, *Impuestos Internos.*

Tax Base

In addition to changing the tax structure, the Salvadoran government has taken steps to increase the number of taxpayers. Numerous administrative reforms have been implemented in order to increase tax revenues. These reforms include the introduction of a system of withholding for the personal income tax, writing new laws to close tax loopholes, reducing the number of exemptions, creating new tax agencies, reorganizing existing agencies and computerizing operations (Trigueros, n.d., pp. 5-8).

Implementation of World Bank Advice

Clearly, the Salvadoran tax reform follows the WB guidelines. The reform changes both the tax structure and the number of taxpayers. The principal changes in the tax structure consist of making the income taxes less progressive and of placing more emphasis on sales taxes, especially the VAT. The attempts to increase the number of taxpayers implement the WB recommendations to make legal and administrative reforms. It seems clear that the WB tax advice guided the Salvadoran tax reform either directly or indirectly through the effect of the advice on other institutions.

IMPACT ON THE DEVELOPMENT PROCESS

Measuring Tax Incidence

Tax incidence is the distribution of the tax burden among persons of different income classes. As indicated in chapter 8, a progressive tax system (in which the percentage of income paid as tax rises with income) is required to satisfy the basic needs of the poor as quickly as possible.

The ideal way to measure tax incidence is to calculate the percentages of income paid for taxes by persons of various levels of income. This measurement results in a table like the following that estimates the tax incidence in the United States for the year 1985. In the table, level 1 represents the 20% of the population with the lowest income, and level 5 represents the 20% with the highest income.

Constructing tax incidence tables like Table 9.3 is the ideal, but it is difficult to do in practice. After using economic theory to predict tax incidence, it is necessary to obtain detailed empirical data in order to assign tax revenues to each income class. Normally, these data are not available in Latin America.

There is another approach that is less accurate than the ideal, but it has the advantage of being feasible. First, economic theory is used to determine whether each tax in the system is progressive or regressive. A useful conclusion of this analysis is that direct taxes are generally progressive and indirect taxes are generally regressive.

The second step of the more feasible approach is to collect empirical data on the percentage of total tax revenue raised by the progressive direct taxes and the percentage raised by regressive indirect taxes. If a

Table 9.3. Tax Incidence in the United States, 1985

*Income Level**	*Effective Tax Rate (%)*
1	33
2	39
3	47
4	50
5	55

Note: *5 = highest income level.
Source: Musgrave and Musgrave (1989, Table 14-1, p. 243).

comparison of the two amounts shows that the majority of revenues is collected by regressive indirect taxes, the tax system is considered to be regressive. If the majority is collected by progressive direct taxes, the system is considered to be progressive.

This approach has its limitations. For example, an increase in the percentage of revenues generated by progressive direct taxes creates the impression that the system has become more progressive. However, Table 9.3 indicates that if the highest income class evades its taxes, and if the other classes pay the increase in revenues, the system actually becomes more regressive in the upper range of incomes even though the percentage of direct tax revenues has increased.

Salvadoran Incidence

Table 9.4 shows the tax revenues of El Salvador by tax for the prereform year of 1990 and the postreform year of 2008. Column (1) lists the main Salvadoran taxes. Columns (2) and (3) show the revenue, and the percentage of total tax revenue, raised by each tax for the two years. The figures written in bold type give the totals of the direct taxes, indirect taxes, and tax revenue from all sources.

Table 9.4 indicates that, according to the simple method of measuring incidence, the tax system has been, and remains, highly regressive. In 1990, 73.1% of total tax revenues were raised by regressive indirect taxes, while only 27.7% was raised by means of progressive direct taxes. In 2008, the percentages were 64.6% and 35.4%, respectively. Regressive indirect tax revenues are almost double the progressive direct tax revenues.

The figures show some progress in reducing the regressivity of the tax system between 1990 and 2008: the percentage of total tax revenue raised

Table 9.4. Tax Revenues of El Salvador 1990, 2008 (Millions of Dollars)

(1)	*(2)*		*(3)*	
	1990		*2008(p)*	
Tax	*Amount*	*%*	*Amount*	*%*
Direct	123.5	27.7	1,021.9	35.4
1. Income	97.1	21.8	1,004.1	34.8
2. Property	16.7	3.7	0	0
3. Transfers of property	9.7	2.2	17.8	0.6
Indirect	326.1	73.1	1,863.2	64.6
4. International trade	96.4	21.4	178.2	6.2
Imports	62.2	14	178.2	6.2
Exports	34.2	7.7	0	0
5. Excise sales	66.6	14.9	95.8	3.3
6. Services	6.9	1.5	0	0
7. Papel sellado	1.3	0.3	0	0
8. Cascade	134.8	30.2	0	0
9. VAT	0	0	1,460.7	50.6
10. Special contribution (FOVIAL)	0	0	65.9	2.3
11. Statistical adjustment	–14.7	–3.3	0	0
12. Other	34.8	7.8	62.6	2.2
Total	449.6	100*	2,885.8	100

Notes: (p) = preliminary. *Error due to rounding.
Source: Banco Central de Reserva de El Salvador. (2008).

by regressive indirect taxes declined from 73.1% to 64.6%, and the percentage raised by progressive direct taxes rose from 27.7% to 35.4%.

The significance of this change depends heavily upon precisely which income classes paid the additional tax revenues. If the highest income class has evaded its taxes, then it is the middle income class that paid the additional direct tax revenues. In this case, a table such as Table 9.3 would show more regressivity in the highest income range, and more progressivity in the low and middle income ranges. This has important implications for political control of the country and satisfying basic needs.

Finally, Table 9.4 shows an impressive increase in total tax revenues from $449.6 million in 1990 to $2885.8 million in 2008. This constitutes an average annual increase in tax revenue of 30%. The question of whether the increase was caused by the WB tax advice is treated below.

Tax Evasion

A study carried out by the United States embassy of El Salvador concluded that there is widespread tax evasion in El Salvador, mainly of the VAT and the tax on business income (cited in CIDAI, 2008, No. 1277, p. 15). According to the study, in 2006 the Salvadoran government captured only 61.1% of the VAT that was due and 41.3% of the tax on business income.

The analytical bulletin published weekly by the Central American University José Simeón Cañas, *Proceso,* argues that the main tax evaders are large businesses because they are the agents who retain taxes for the government. Small businesses are mainly subsistence enterprises that operate in the informal sector, and, as such, do not pay taxes. Large businesses are generally owned by the highest income class.

According to *Proceso,* a mechanism commonly used by large companies to evade taxes is the use of two sets of accounting books, one real and the other fictitious. The fictitious books show fewer commercial transactions (and less VAT due) and lower profits (CIDAI, 2008, No. 1278, p. 15). If the government wanted to discover the trickery, states *Proceso,* it could easily do so. It would simply have to crosscheck the receipts presented by the firm that sells with those presented by the firm that buys. And why doesn't the government crosscheck? Because large business persons "own" the government, and because the government is "at their service" (CIDAI, 2008, No. 1278, p. 15).

Chapter 8 argued that the well-to-do have both the economic incentive and the political power to evade their taxes. If the large business owners are in fact the principal tax evaders, then Table 9.4 underestimates the regressivity of the tax system and overestimates the reduction in regressivity.

The changes recorded in Table 9.2 reinforce the point that the tax system has been made more regressive in the highest income range. There we saw that the maximum marginal rates on the income taxes were greatly reduced, and that the national property tax, the gift tax and the inheritance tax have all been eliminated. These changes mainly benefit the highest income class.

Table 9.5. Default Indicators

(Total External Debt) / (Exports of Goods and Services)								
Country	*1980*	*1982*	*1984*	*1986*	*1988*	*1990*	*1992*	*1994*
El Salvador	71.1	150.1	161.9	143.5	180.4	171.6	135.1	93.4
Mexico	250.1	311.5	291.3	422.7	309.1	238.8	238.6	228.1
(Total Debt Service)/(Exports of Goods and Services) (Including Remittances of Workers)								
El Salvador	7.5	13.6	21.6	32.2	18.3	16.7	13.9	14.5
Mexico	47.8	56.8	52.1	54.2	48.2	25.9	44.3	33.9

Source: World Bank (1990, 1996, World Debt Tables 1990-91 and 1996).

International Debt Crisis?

The objective of the WB was to increase tax revenues of developing countries in order to resolve the international debt crisis. Was there an international debt crisis in El Salvador? Table 9.5 suggests that the answer to this question is "no." The table lists two crucial indicators of the ability of a country to pay its external debt, the ratios of (total external debt/ exports) and (debt service/exports). These ratios indicate whether a country is earning sufficient foreign exchange through its exports to pay off its debt.

Precisely when is a country in danger of default? "A measure greater than 200% in the level of total external debt to exports or a debt service to export ratio over 40% is unhealthy, pointing to great pressure on exports for debt payments and leaving little capital for other investment" (Franco, 2003, pp. 89-90).

The table shows that the Salvadoran ratios never exceeded these criteria. The highest value for the ratio (total external debt/exports) was 180.4 in 1988, 20 points below the criterion of 200. The average value for this ratio is 138, more than 60 points below the criterion. The maximum value of the ratio (total debt service/exports of goods and services) was 32.2 in 1986, almost 8 points below the criterion of 40, and its average value was only 17.

In contrast, Mexico—the country that declared a moratorium on the payments of its international debt in 1982—had a ratio of (total external debt/exports) that exceeded 200 in all the years listed in the table, and the ratio (debt service/exports) exceeded the criterion of 40 in six of the eight years listed. The average value of the Mexican ratio (286.3) was more than double the ratio of El Salvador (138.4). The average of Mexico's ratio of (debt service/exports) for the listed years (45.4) was 2.5 times greater than the Salvadoran average (17.3). Hence, the data indicates that El Salvador was not forced by an external debt crisis to adopt the tax advice of the WB. We must look elsewhere for an explanation.

Even though El Salvador was not desperate to increase its revenues in order to pay its international debt, the government was in need of additional revenues in order to carry out its normal functions. Historically, the tax effort of El Salvador as measured by the ratio (tax revenues/gross domestic product), has been one of the lowest in Latin America. In the year 2000, the El Salvador's ratio was 10.2% while the average ratio for all of Latin America was 12.8% (Trigueros, n.d., Box 1, p. 4). For industrialized countries, the average tax effort was 32% (World Bank, 1991, Table 1, p. 16).

During the 1990s, the extreme inequality and poverty of El Salvador were placing heavy pressure on the government to provide more basic goods and services. The government also needed to rebuild the public infrastructure after the civil war that lasted 12 years and terminated in 1991. It appears that El Salvador adopted the WB tax advice for increasing revenue, not to avoid default on its international debt payments, but rather to provide the public goods and services that the country badly needed. The question is not whether the country needs to increase tax revenues, but whether it should do so by means of regressive taxation.

More Revenues?

Chapter 8 argues that the principle objective of WB tax advice is to raise revenues. Has the WB been successful in raising Salvadoran tax revenues? Table 9.4 showed a substantial increase in revenues between 1990 and 2008. Table 9.6 examines the revenue growth in greater detail. Column (2) shows total tax revenues for the years 1980-2005. El Salvador adopted the U.S. dollar as its official currency in 2001, and since the exchange rate was approximately 9 Salvadoran Colones per dollar, the data show a sharp decline in that year.

Column (3) of Table 9.6 shows the annual growth of tax revenues. The last three rows of Column (3) show that for the period before the tax reform, 1980-1990, tax revenues grew at an average annual rate of 12.6%. During the first five years of the reform (1990-1995), the average annual growth rate rose to 26.1%. However during the subsequent period, 1996-2005, the average annual growth rate fell sharply to 8%.[1]

It appears that the reform spurred growth for five years, but then growth fell to only two thirds of the prereform growth rate. If the revenue growth continues at its relatively low rate in the future, the long-run effect

Table 9.6. Salvadoran Revenues and Spending

(1)	(2)	(3)	(4)	(5)	(6)
Year	*Tax Revenues**	*%Δ Revenue*	*Health + Education**	*(4) / (2)*	*%Δ Spending*
2005	2,132.8	22.80%	753.9	0.35	10.35%
2004	1,736.8	3.44%	683.2	0.39	5.79%
2003	1,679.1	9.58%	645.8	0.38	–4.71%
2002	1,532.3	10.45%	677.7	0.44	0.10%
2001	1,387.3	...	677.0	0.49	...
2000	12,484.9	6.49%	3,353.2	0.27	13.66%
1999	11,723.8	8.71%	2,950.2	0.25	7.68%
1998	10,784.0	4.79%	2,739.9	0.25	–23.83%
1997	10,290.8	–2.91%	3,597.3	0.35	11.58%
1996	10,599.1	5.31%	3,224.1	0.30	19.41%
1995	10,064.5	32.27%	2,700.0	0.27	22.48%
1994	7,609.1	25.32%	2,204.5	0.29	31.75%
1993	6,071.5	23.51%	1,673.3	0.28	36.66%
1992	4,915.7	19.34%	1,224.4	0.25	12.86%
1991	4,119.2	26.90%	1,084.9	0.26	13.78%
1990	3,246.1	29.33%	953.5	0.29	14.76%
1989	2,509.9	–4.30%	830.9	0.33	13.51%
1988	2,622.8	2.69%	732.0	0.28	4.48%
1987	2,554.1	–6.92%	700.6	0.27	13.48%
1986	2,743.9	61.52%	617.4	0.23	13.47%
1985	1,698.8	23.89%	544.1	0.32	10.28%
1984	1,371.2	24.54%	493.4	0.36	15.44%
1983	1,101.0	14.33%	427.4	0.39	3.39%
1982	963.0	–3.90%	413.4	0.43	–2.43%
1981	1,002.1	1.29%	423.7	0.42	–3.84%
1980	980.3		440.6	0.45	
Average 1996-2005		8.0%		0.35	4.4%
Average 1990-1995		26.1%		0.27	22.0%
Average 1980-1989		12.6%		0.35	7.5%

Note: *Millions of Colones, 1980-2000. Millions of Dollars, 2001-2005.
Sources: International Monetary Fund (various years), Author's calculations.

of the tax reform on the growth of revenues may be small or even negative. If so, the reform will have introduced significantly regressive elements into the tax structure in exchange for nothing more than a temporary increase in revenues.

More Spending for Basic Goods and Services?

We saw in chapter 8 that the WB's justification for advising poor countries to adopt regressive tax reforms is that focusing on the expenditure side of the budget is sufficient for satisfying basic needs. Column (4) of Table 9.6 presents the evolution of expenditures for health and education over the years 1980-2005. Basic health and education are undoubtedly key services for increasing the productivity of low-income workers. Two limitations of considering only health and education are that other basic needs are ignored, and, as noted in chapter 3, government expenditures for education and health often benefit the nonpoor. Once again, 2001 shows a sharp decline because of El Salvador's adoption of the U.S. dollar as its official currency.

Column (5) shows the ratio, (expenditures for health and education)/(tax revenues). The last three rows of column (5) compare the averages of the ratio over distinct periods of time. Before the reform (1980-1989), El Salvador spent an average of 35% of its tax revenue on health and education. During the first years of the reform (1990-1996) the average ratio fell to 0.27, and then it returned to its original level of 0.35.

The small variation suggests that the practice of the Salvadoran government is to spend a more or less constant percentage of tax revenues for health and education. This does not indicate a change of priorities in favor of satisfying basic needs in order to create a more inclusive development process. On the contrary, if tax revenues continue growing at their relatively slow pace, expenditures for health and education are likely to grow more slowly than before the reform.

Column (6) shows the percentage increase in health and education expenditures for each year. Like tax revenues, the expenditures show a period of rapid growth at the beginning of the reform (1990-1995), but then the growth rate diminishes substantially. The last three rows of the column show that expenditures grew an average of 22% during the years 1990-1995, but then the growth rate fell to 4.5%, a rate that was far less than the prereform rate of 7.5%. This coincides with the empirical evidence of chapter 8 that indicated that expenditures for health and education have increased "slowly."

Column (6) gives the "nominal" increases in expenditures for health and education, not the "real" increases that take into account the rate of inflation and the capacity of a dollar to purchase the services. During the years 1996-2005, expenditures for health and education grew an average of 4.4% per year, but the inflation rates for health and education in El Salvador were 4.5% and 9.23%, respectively (Banco Central de Reserva de El Salvador, 2008). Given that prices of education and health services rose more rapidly than expenditures, the purchasing power of the currency diminished and fewer needs for these services were satisfied.

CONCLUSION

The WB justifies its policy of advising regressive taxation by assuming that regressive taxes will increase government revenues, and that the additional revenues will then be used to satisfy basic needs. Chapter 8 questioned the logic of the assumptions and presented evidence that supports the hypothesis that it is progressive—not regressive—taxation that best satisfies basic needs and generates inclusive development.

This chapter's case study of El Salvador throws further doubt upon the validity of the WB's assumptions and strategy. Implementation of the WB tax advice in El Salvador was followed by lower long-term growth rates of both tax revenues and central government expenditures for health and education. If this trend continues, the satisfaction of basic needs and the implementation of an inclusive development process could be slowed or stymied.

A key issue is the long-term effect of the WB tax advice on class structure. In El Salvador, less progressive tax rates on personal income, a lower tax rate on business income, and continuing tax evasion seem to have lowered the present and future tax burden on the highest income class that rules El Salvador.

Professor Alan Tait begins his book on wealth taxation with the following observation:

> Taxation is never popular. Taxation of wealth is for many the least popular of all taxes. Such a tax alters the very stuff of society: the family, death, and the historical continuity of houses, land, and all personal property. Wealth taxes alter the relations of groups and persons in the social hierarchy. Those who own land, those who have family businesses, those who buy stocks and shares, and those who own nothing, all have their relative positions altered by taxes on wealth. These taxes are a powerful engine for change. Excise taxation seems almost frivolous by comparison. (Tait, 1967, p. 1)

The tax reform in El Salvador has been carried out by ARENA, the political party that was explicitly founded to represent the interests of the oligarchy. If Professor Tait is correct, eliminating the taxes on property, inheritances and gifts have been ARENA's most important step to secure El Salvador's inequality for the indefinite future. Did the oligarchy seize upon WB pressures for tax reform—including tax simplification—to eliminate these key taxes and to secure the status quo for the indefinite future?

The satisfaction of basic needs in a short period of time and the generation of an inclusive development process require progressive taxation. Salvadoran policymakers could best achieve this objective by making the income taxes more progressive, by lowering the VAT rate, by combating evasion, and by reinstituting the national property tax, the gift tax, and the inheritance tax at progressive rates.

The people of El Salvador must combat centuries of tradition in which government has often served the interests of the oligarchs rather than the common good, and they must function in an environment in which the defense of privilege has been extremely violent. Success depends upon receiving much support. The citizens/clients must encourage politicians with their votes and their voices. The World Bank should adopt the tax objective of inclusive development, and it should advise progressive taxation and using the tax revenues to satisfy the basic needs of the poor in a short period of time. The following chapter considers the role that developed countries and international institutions can play through international aid.

NOTE

1. The 8% figure is the unweighted average of the mean growth rates for the years 1996-2000 and 2001-2005.

CHAPTER 10

DECENTRALIZING THE FOREIGN AID OF THE UNITED STATES

"Donors should strengthen the critical relationships among policymakers, providers and clients."

—World Bank

INTRODUCTION

Chapter 1 indicated that many Latin Americans are living on less than $2 a day. Some are living far below this poverty line. Countless more are living in "near poverty" on $3, $5, or $10 a day. The financial requirements for satisfying the basic needs that incorporate all Latin Americans into the development process within a short period of time are challenging for Latin American countries plagued by extreme inequality. This raises the subject of foreign aid from the United States to Latin America for satisfying the basic needs of the poor and generating an inclusive development process.

Foreign aid from developed to underdeveloped countries has been at times a spectacular success and at other times a miserable failure. Through these experiences, the international community has progressed in understanding what makes aid more effective. Research and experi-

Decentralization for Satisfying Basic Needs: An Economic Guide for Policymakers, 2nd Edition
pp. 141–163

ence teach that the effectiveness of foreign aid can be increased by selecting recipient countries that are able and willing to use it well, and by decentralizing planning and expenditure decisions from donors to these recipients.

The purpose of this chapter is to explore the role of decentralization in making foreign aid more effective in satisfying the basic needs of the poor and generating an inclusive development process. In the first section of the chapter, the term "foreign aid" is defined, and the amounts of aid are described. Next, the model of service delivery (chapters 3-4) is expanded to encompass foreign aid and to yield guidelines for maximizing its effectiveness in satisfying the basic needs of the poor. Then a new approach to foreign aid by the United States—The Millennium Challenge Account (MCA)—is described and evaluated in light of the model. The chapter concludes with an evaluation of MCA and recommendations for policymakers.

WHAT IS FOREIGN AID?[1]

The term "foreign aid" is usually associated with *Net Official Development Assistance* (ODA). This comprises grants plus concessional loans that have at least a 25% grant component and that are normally targeted to the poorest countries. *Net* ODA excludes assistance for military purposes and for more advanced developing and transitional countries. *Gross* ODA includes these expenditures. The focus of this chapter is development assistance to poor countries as measured by Net ODA.

ODA can be divided into bilateral and multilateral components. Bilateral assistance is administered by agencies of donor governments such as the U.S. Agency for International Development (USAID). Multilateral assistance is funded by agencies such as the United Nations Development Program (UNDP) and the World Bank. Of all official development assistance, roughly one third is multilateral, and two thirds is bilateral.

Some bilateral aid is "tied"—it must be used to procure goods and services from the donor country. Studies have shown that tied aid reduces the value of that assistance by 25-40% through raising the prices of inputs (Shah, 2008).

AMOUNTS OF OFFICIAL DEVELOPMENT ASSISTANCE

Commitment

When the world's governments met at the Earth summit in Rio de Janeiro in 1992, they adopted a program for action under the auspices of the United Nations Agenda 21 that included an ODA target of 0.7% of Gross National Income (GNI) for rich nations. The "rich nations" are 22 members of the OECD (Organization of Economic Cooperation and Development), known as the DAC (Development Assistance Committee) (Shah, 2008).

Amounts

Table 10.1 indicates the amounts of Net ODA in current U.S. dollars given by the 22 richest countries of the OECD for the years 2000, 2007 and 2008. The table shows that only five Scandinavian countries met the aid target of 0.7% of GNI in 2008, and that they have consistently done so since at least 2000. The United States gave the largest amount of aid in absolute dollar terms (almost twice the amount of the second largest donor, Germany), but the smallest amount in terms of the percentage of GNI. U.S. aid has increased steadily since 2000 in both dollar and percentage terms.

The OECD reports that for the years 2006-2007, the United States gave an average Gross ODA of $1.916 billion to Latin America (OECD, 2009b). This constituted 9.1% of its entire Gross ODA. The top ten recipients of Gross ODA granted by the United States included only one Latin American country, Colombia.

A UNICEF publication estimated that in the year 1999, there existed a shortfall in public spending of about $80 billion a year (1995 prices) to achieve universal provision of basic services, with around $216 billion required and only $136 billion being spent (United Nations, 2000, Box 4.5, p. 79). Other studies estimated that external aid would have needed to increase by $40-100 billion a year. One frequently cited estimate by the UN Zedillo Commission called for an additional $50 billion a year, a number that is consistent with the World Bank's estimate (United Nations, 2003, p. 146). In 2000, the DAC gave approximately $53 billion in ODA. To eliminate the shortfall, it would have been necessary to approximately double this aid.

TRADITIONAL CRITICISMS OF U.S. AID

The United States has been criticized for giving an amount of official development assistance (0.18%) that falls far below the target of 0.7% of GNI agreed upon at the Monterrey Conference. Second, in 2007, 87% of U.S. aid was bilateral, and a very high percentage of bilateral aid (71.6%

Table 10.1. Net Official Development Assistance, 2000-2008

	2008		*2007*		*2000*	
Country	*ODA USD Million Current*	*ODA/GNI %*	*ODA USD Million Current*	*ODA/GNI %*	*ODA USD Million Current*	*ODA/GNI %*
Australia	3,166	0.34	2,669	0.32	995	0.27
Austria	1,681	0.42	1,808	0.50	461	0.25
Belgium	2,381	0.47	1,953	0.43	812	0.36
Canada	4,725	0.32	4,080	0.29	1,722	0.25
Denmark	2,800	0.82	2,562	0.81	1,664	1.06
Finland	1,139	0.43	981	0.39	371	0.31
France	10,957	0.39	9,884	0.38	4,221	0.33
Germany	13,910	0.38	12,291	0.37	5,034	0.27
Greece	693	0.20	501	0.16	216	0.19
Ireland	1,325	0.58	1,192	0.55	239	0.30
Italy	4,444	0.20	3,971	0.19	1,368	0.13
Japan	9,362	0.18	7,679	0.17	13,062	0.27
Luxembourg	409	0.92	376	0.91	116	0.70
Netherlands	6,993	0.80	6,224	0.81	3,075	0.82
New Zealand	346	0.30	320	0.27	116	0.26
Norway	3,967	0.88	3,728	0.95	1,264	0.80
Portugal	614	0.27	471	0.22	261	0.26
Spain	6,686	0.43	5,140	0.37	1,321	0.24
Sweden	4,730	0.98	4,339	0.93	1,813	0.81
Switzerland	2,016	0.41	1,685	0.37	888	0.34
United Kingdom	11,409	0.43	9,849	0.35	4,458	0.31
United States	26,008	0.18	21,787	0.16	9,581	0.10
Average country effort		0.47		0.45		0.39

Note: The data for 2008 are preliminary.
Sources: OECD (2009a) and Shah (2008).

for the year 1999) was "tied" to the purchase of U.S. goods and services (Shah, 2008). Third, a high percentage of U.S. aid focuses on achieving strategic objectives rather than satisfying the basic needs of the poor. For example, in 2007 the top four recipients of gross ODA were countries that were important in fighting the wars on terrorism and illegal drugs: Iraq,

Afghanistan, Sudan, and Colombia (OECD, 2009b). A related issue is that subsidies for U.S. agriculture and other products together with trade barriers more than offset the benefits of aid by hurting markets in developing countries, and by making it difficult for them to export their way out of poverty (Shah, 2008).

DECENTRALIZATION MODEL FOR AID[2]

Figure 10.1 expands the model of service delivery to account for foreign aid. The figure is broken down into two major sections, donors and recipients. Three agents of the donor countries are involved in delivering foreign aid to recipient countries: taxpayers and interest groups, politicians and policymakers, and aid agencies. Viewing aid as a "public good," taxpayers and interest groups voice their demand for foreign aid to their politicians and policymakers. The politicians and policymakers design aid policy, tax the citizens, and transfer the revenues to the aid agencies that distribute and manage it.

Within recipient countries, the familiar three categories of agents drive the use of foreign aid: the poor, the politicians and policymakers, and the providers. The system should operate as described in chapter 3. The Poor "voice" their needs to politicians and policymakers who respond by planning a "compact" with service providers for delivering basic goods and services to the poor. The goods and services are delivered by providers in

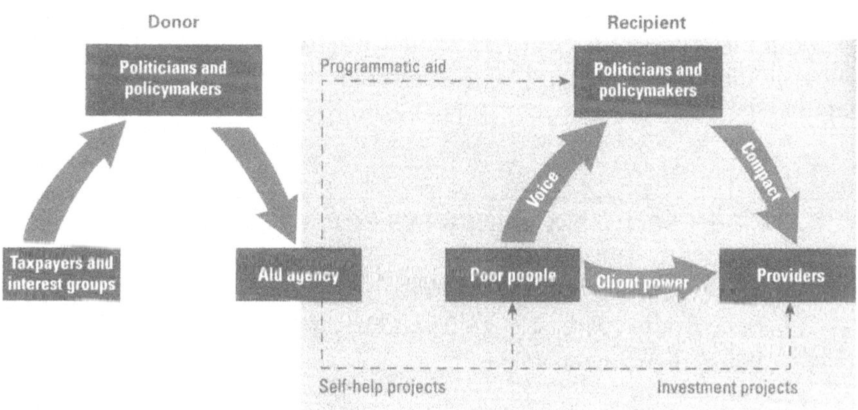

Source: World Bank (2003, p. 204).

Figure 10.1. Decentralization model of foreign aid.

consultation with the poor and with their participation. Provider outcomes are monitored by the poor, the policymakers and the aid agencies.

The figure shows that donors can distribute aid to three different recipients. "Programmatic aid" can be given directly to the politicians and policymakers. Money for "self-help projects" such as roads can be given directly to the poor. Money for "investment projects" such as health clinics or schools can be given directly to the providers. An important question is: Which recipient is most effective in satisfying the basic needs of the poor?

Principles for Effective Official Development Assistance

How can official development assistance be made most effective in satisfying the basic needs of the poor and generating an inclusive development process? Box 10.1 lists six principles for making aid effective that are derived from the model of Figure 10.1. The short answer, given in principles 1-2, is: give the money to countries with effective service delivery systems and let them spend it as they will. Principles 4-6 speak of ways to strengthen service delivery systems in recipient countries. The following pages explain in greater detail how the principles may be implemented.

First Principle: Choose Recipient Countries Well

Effective Delivery System. The first principle of effective aid is to help countries with an effective system for delivering basic goods and services to the poor. The service delivery model indicates what this means: the poor should have voice and client power; politicians and policymakers should be willing and able to respond to the Poor by formulating an effec-

BOX 10.1. SIX PRINCIPLES FOR EFFECTIVE AID

1. Choose recipient countries well;
2. Decentralize planning and spending;
3. Strengthen citizen voice;
4. Let providers manage;
5. Strengthen client power; and
6. For weak states, balance urgent service needs with system building

tive compact. Providers should be capable of managing projects in consultation with the poor. There should be a system of monitoring outcomes and of using the results to institute continual improvement.

Shift in Emphasis. Focusing on the quality of a country's service delivery system marks a radical departure from the traditional approach to giving foreign aid. The traditional approach is for donors to design development projects and establish conditions to assure that the money is spent appropriately. The shift is from projects to systems, and from management by aid agencies to management by recipients.

A reason for the shift in emphasis is that foreign aid is "fungible." This means that recipient governments may use financial aid to replace their own spending. Aid for education may be used to reduce own-expenditures for education. Taxes may be cut, the money may be moved out of education and into some other sector, or it may be stolen. The net effect on education spending may be small, or zero, or even negative (if the recipient government's spending cuts are greater than the amount of aid received).

Empirical studies find that the impact of aid on the spending of recipient governments for sectors such as education varies widely between countries (World Bank 2003, pp. 61-74).

In one striking study of 14 underdeveloped countries, the net effect of $1 of aid for education and health was a net *reduction* in education and health spending of 6.5 cents. Here, aid for education and health led to *less* total spending on education and health! At the other extreme, a study of Indonesia concluded that $1 in aid for agriculture increased spending for agriculture by 92 cents.

Overall, the fungibility of foreign aid seems to vary widely and in ways that are difficult to predict. Aid would not be fully fungible if the recipient governments were spending less on the funded sector than the amount of aid, but this is likely to be an exceptional case. Almost all studies conclude that foreign aid is generally fungible, and that it is often very fungible or completely fungible. The World Bank concludes that "the safest assumption for donors is that they are, more or less, financing whatever the (recipient) government chooses to do" (World Bank 2003, p. 74). Since recipient governments are in effect going to do whatever they want with aid, the best policy is to focus not on funding individual projects, but rather on funding governments that are able and willing to use it well, i.e., the governments that have built effective service delivery systems.

Empirical Evidence. There is impressive evidence that helping countries with strong institutions and policies increases the impact of aid on poverty reduction. One study concludes that a $10 billion increase in official development assistance distributed according to the existing aid allocation could raise 7 million people out of poverty. However, if the additional $10 billion were reallocated to countries with strong policies and institutions, 25 million people would be raised out of poverty (Collier & Dollar, 1998, cited in World Bank 1998, p. 46). This suggests that choosing countries well may increase the number of people lifted out of poverty almost fourfold.

Further evidence is provided by the experience of the World Bank. Public investment projects financed by the World Bank in, for example, roads, power, and education, were 86% successful in countries with good management. In countries with weak policies and institutions, the corresponding figure was a much lower 48% (World Bank, 2003, p. 15). Choosing countries well practically doubled the success rate of World Bank projects.

This is not to say that "well-managed" countries are perfect. Almost by definition, all underdeveloped countries have weaknesses in their service delivery systems. For example, the voice and the client power of the poor are weak in virtually all countries, both developed and underdeveloped. Hence, labeling a country "well-managed" does not imply that there is no room for improvement. Instead, the first principle states that aid will be *relatively* effective in underdeveloped countries with *relatively* strong service delivery systems. Aid is more likely to be wasted in countries with relatively weak service delivery systems. Still, all countries need to improve. Some of the principles that follow are intended to help countries—both "strong" and "weak"—to improve their capacity to satisfy the basic needs of the poor.

Second Principle: Decentralize Planning and Spending

Give General Budget Support. Having chosen recipients well, the second principle of effective aid is to let them decide how best to use the money. The most effective approach is to simply give general budget support to well-managed countries and to rely on them to plan and to spend the money in the way that satisfies as many basic needs as possible. Well managed countries know their needs and circumstances far better than international aid agencies, and they are better able to spend the money well. Besides, fungibility means that aid recipients are going to do pretty much what they want with the money anyway—either directly or indirectly. Multitudinous conditions imposed by aid agencies are in vain. Another advantage of simple budget support is that it reduces transaction costs and frees recipients to spend more of their time and energy on satisfying basic needs.

What assurance do donors have that the money will not be wasted? The best assurance is that the recipient countries are well managed. They have a track record for satisfying basic needs effectively. Another assurance comes from monitoring outcomes (as opposed to inputs) and using them as a basis for deciding whether donors will continue to give aid in the future. Ideally, outcomes that serve as a basis for continuing aid will include not only achievements in delivering basic goods and services, but also achievements in improving service delivery systems.

To Politicians and Policymakers. The World Bank argues that the service delivery compact between policymakers and providers of developing nations is strengthened by delivering aid to politicians and policymakers, and not directly to the poor or to service providers (World Bank, 2003, pp. 204-206). If aid is not delivered to the politicians and policymakers, they lose control over expenditures, and over-all planning and management is lost. Incoherent spending allocations and uneven coverage ensue. For example, if many donors transfer money directly to providers in order to build health clinics, too many clinics may be built at the cost of other, more pressing needs. Also, if the politicians and policymakers have not been involved, the money and staff required to operate the clinics over the long-term (after the aid terminates) may not be forthcoming.

Curiously, the World Bank overlooks the theory of public finance which suggests that the best way to strengthen the compact would be to give the money directly to the poor. This would enhance the voice of the poor by giving them the money necessary to demand the public goods and services that they need from the government and to pay the taxes necessary to fund them. Having invested their money in the goods and services, the poor would be intensely interested in assuring their quality, that is, client power would be increased. Perhaps the World Bank adopts its position because donors would not be willing to fund this approach. If money is given directly to the politicians and policymakers, efforts to increase the voice and client power of the poor should be redoubled (principles 3 and 5).

Third Principle: Strengthen Citizen Voice

The voice of the poor in developing countries is generally extremely weak. Instead of the poor voicing their needs to their government and participating in constructing strategies to satisfy those needs, they become passive objects of meager and often misguided assistance. How can donors use aid to strengthen citizen voice?

This is a very hard nut to crack. Sometimes, powerful interests do not want to give voice to the poor. Sometimes, the poor are not accustomed to expressing their needs. Sometimes they are acculturated to be passive and silent. Nevertheless, because voice is so important in satisfying basic needs effectively, donors have attempted to strengthen it in many ways (World Bank 2003, pp. 209-211).

Aid has been made conditional upon having instituted democratic elections—upon having made the reform, not promised it. Aid has helped to pay the costs of free elections, to send election observers, and to provide technical support to election administrators. Donors have sponsored forums to air public debates on television and radio. They have supported more timely information to voters and the greater use of local languages.

Another donor approach to enhancing voice has been to promote participatory processes in the development of poverty reduction strategies and budgetary processes. Donors have supported governments that invite the donors and a wide range of civil society to participate in reviewing plans for future public expenditures. Likewise, they have supported governments that present a national development strategy that is supported by broad ownership and well-defined sector priorities.

Fourth Principle: Let Provider Organizations Manage

Donors can affect the management of provider organization in recipient countries in at least three ways: by fragmenting aid into a large number of donor projects, by the choice of activities, and by the choice of inputs.

Fragmenting aid into a large number of donor projects can impose very high transaction costs on recipients as they spend large amounts of time and energy satisfying diverse conditions imposed by a multitude of donor countries. On the other hand, pooling the aid of many donors into a single or a few packages reduces transaction costs and frees recipients to spend more time and energy on satisfying basic needs. Having selected well-managed countries, it is best to let them use their skills to satisfy basic needs.

Donors can also reduce the effectiveness of aid by distorting the choice of inputs and activities. For example, donors tend to invest too many resources in training, and they buy far more technical assistance (and project vehicles) than the providers would buy if they were managing the money (World Bank, 2003, pp. 207-208). The result is that the effectiveness of aid is reduced. Letting providers manage the expenditures also builds their capacity to do so.

Fifth Principle: Increase Client Power

The relationship between the beneficiary and service provider tends to be weak in developing countries. Donors can enhance client power by pooling support and distributing it transparently. This helps citizens to monitor the use of aid and to avoid capture by elites. Impact evaluations should be built into aid projects. The aid compact should contain verifiable indicators that can measure performance outcomes (not inputs). Donors can encourage citizen monitoring of service providers such as citizen report cards that grade the delivery of basic goods and services, and by surveys that track public expenditures. Transparent mechanisms should allow donors to signal the conditions for a recipient to expect an increase or reduction in aid.

Sixth Principle: For Weak States, Balance System Building With Needs

The last principle for effective foreign aid is extremely important because most underdeveloped countries do not have strong systems of delivering basic goods and services to the poor. Voice and client power are not strong, but weak—often extremely weak. Compacts are likewise weak not only because voice and client power fail to give input, but also because many developing countries lack the capacity or the will to plan and administer basic needs programs.

What should aid donors do about the majority of underdeveloped countries that have weak service delivery systems? The short answer is to focus on building the delivery system that is lacking and restrict financial assistance to meeting urgent needs for basic goods and services.

In the few poor countries where the public sector is already effective in satisfying basic needs, the task of foreign aid is straightforward: simple budgetary support is likely to be most beneficial. But financing more of the same in developing governments that are not effective at providing public services is unlikely to be beneficial. The need here is to deemphasize financial assistance and to focus on building the service delivery system.

One way to do this is for aid agencies of donor countries to draw on their experience and their empirical studies to assist with policy analysis, share technical expertise, train domestic actors, and stimulate policy debate in civil society. In most cases these are relatively low-cost measures, so there is no contradiction with the strong message that most finance should go to poor countries with strong delivery systems.

The role of financial aid to dysfunctional countries is to address urgent, short-term service needs. Effective programs like Mexico's *Oportunidades* can be supported, as well as effective governmental units like the *presidencias municipales comunitarias* of Tlaxcala, Mexico. In other cases, it may be necessary to bypass the state and give the money directly to the poor for self-help projects or to non-state actors such as NGOs. Nongovernmental channels for service delivery can play an important role in the short-run, but aiding them should be seen as a transitional strategy to strengthen state capacity in the long term. Properly managed, financial aid to non-state agents can encourage better public sectors through demonstration effects of experimentation, innovation and evaluation. As strong delivery systems are developed, donors can shift toward general budget support of the central government.

MILLENNIUM CHALLENGE ACCOUNT[3]

Purpose

The United States has instituted a new system of providing official development assistance (ODA) that will impact the satisfaction of basic needs and the generation of a more inclusive development process. The new system, called the Millennium Challenge Account (MCA), increases the amount of aid to developing countries, but also makes it conditional upon the achievement of certain outcomes called "performance indicators." Seventeen indicators are used to evaluate performance in three broad policy categories: ruling justly, investing in people, and encouraging economic freedom. The MCA was first announced by President George W. Bush in March 2002 and first implemented in January 2004.

Amount

The original proposal by President Bush was to ramp up ODA by *an additional* $5 billion per year within 3 years, an amount that would have doubled ODA. The president lived up to this commitment by submitting budget requests to the Congress for the MCA of $1.3 billion in 2004 followed by $3.3 billion and $5 billion in the next two fiscal years. However, the proposal met with funding resistance from the Congress immediately. In 2004, Congress only authorized $1.0 billion, which was fully appropriated. In 2005, Congress only authorized $2.3 billion and appropriated only $1.5 billion. In 2006, Congress authorized the full $5 billion but appropriated only $1.77 billion. The funding problem in these early years arose partly from lobbying to ensure that appropriations for the MCC would not reduce funding for other aid programs, and from budget constraints generated by the war on terrorism, especially in Iraq and Afghanistan (Rieffel & Fox, 2008, p. 7). The Obama Administration has requested $1.425 billion to fund the MCA during 2010. This represents a 63% increase over the amount enacted for the agency in 2009.

To date, the MCA has signed compacts with 18 countries totaling $6.3 billion over 5 years, averaging about $350 million per country. Over 70%

of MCA investments are in infrastructure and agricultural development. In addition, it has awarded $440 million to 19 countries for "threshold" programs that aim to help promising countries improve their indicator scores and qualify for aid.

MCA is currently working with seven countries in Latin America. It has 5-year compacts with El Salvador, Honduras, and Nicaragua, totaling more than $850 million. MCA also has 2-year threshold agreements with Paraguay, Guyana, and Peru, totaling an additional $107 million. Colombia was selected as compact-eligible in 2008 (MCC, Latin America).

Administration

The MCA is administered by a new government corporation called the Millennium Challenge Corporation (MCC). The MCC is charged with supporting innovative strategies and ensuring accountability for measurable results. The Corporation attempts to optimize efficiency in contracting, program implementation, and personnel. The corporation is supervised by a board of directors composed of the secretary of state, the secretary of treasury, the U.S. trade representative, and the administrator of USAID. In addition, the chief executive officer and four public members are appointed by the president of the United States with the advice and consent of the U.S. Senate. The secretary of state is the chair of the board and the secretary of treasury is the vice chair. Staff is drawn from a variety of government and non-government agencies.

Eligibility for Benefits

Per Capita Income

The first criterion for receiving development aid from MCA is per capita income. Since performance on the indicators tends to rise with income, two categories of income are used. For the fiscal year 2009, low income countries have a per capita income less than or equal to $1,785, and lower middle income countries have a per capita income greater than $1,785 and less than or equal to $3,705 (MCC, Guide, p. 2). Countries within these income limits are considered "candidates" to receive MCC aid. The income limits are in harmony with the classifications of low and lower middle income countries established by the World Bank.

Indicators

In addition to per capita income, 17 performance indicators are used to select beneficiaries. The indicators are indexes that combine many factors in an attempt to measure the capacity to use foreign aid well. The indicators are grouped in one of three categories: ruling justly, investing in people, and encouraging economic freedom. Specific indicators are chosen because of the relative quality and objectivity of their data, country coverage, public availability, and correlation with growth and poverty reduction. The indicators are preferably developed by independent agencies, and they are in constant evolution. For example, the MCC is trying to find an education indicator that better measures the *quality* of education.

At the risk of oversimplification, Table 10.2 provides a brief list of the indicators and the factors upon which they are based. Appendix A provides a more complete list of factors and the agencies that generate them. A still more complete list of factors and the relationships of each indicator to growth and poverty reduction is available on the MCA web site (MCC, Guide, pp. 7-35).

Use of Indicators

Because a straight ranking determined by adding together the scores for all seventeen indicators might allow exceptional performance in some areas to outweigh dismal performance in others, countries will qualify as better performers only if they demonstrate commitment in all three categories. To do this, they must score above the median in their income peer group on half of the indicators in each of the three categories. In addition, all recipients must pass the test for corruption, and a country may be determined ineligible if it performs substantially below average on any indicator (i.e., the bottom 25th percentile) and has not taken appropriate measures to address the shortcoming.

Qualifying as a better performer does not guarantee MCA support. The board of directors makes a final recommendation to the president. The board is guided primarily by country performance on the indicators, but it is also empowered to take account of data gaps, lags, trends, or other material information, including leadership. A country that passes the indicator test may still be excluded for extremely poor performance for an indicator. MCC can also identify for special transition support called threshold programs a small number of countries that barely miss the list of better performers. In these cases, regular development assistance can be made available to improve their indicator performance.

Decentralization

MCA decentralizes planning and spending. The United States does not dictate how the aid money is to be spent. Instead, each candidate

Table 10.2. Millennium Challenge Corporation Indicators

Indicator	*Factors*
I. Ruling Justly Category	
1. Civil liberties	1. Freedom of expression, association, and organization
2. Political rights	2. Freedom to form political parties and to participate in fair elections
3. Voice and accountability	3. Media independence; institutional protection of civil liberties and political rights
4. Government effectiveness	4. Competency and independence of government; quality of public services
5. Rule of law	5. Effectiveness, independence and predictability of the judiciary; enforceability of contracts
6. Control of corruption	6. Frequency of additional payments; effects on business environment; state capture by elites
II. Investing in People Category	
1. Public expenditures on health	1. Total expenditures on health by government at all levels divided by GDP
2. Immunization rates	2. The average of DPT_3 and measles immunization rates for the most recent year available
3. Total public expenditure on primary education	3. Total expenditures on primary education by government at all levels divided by GDP
4. Girls' primary completion rate	4. The number of female students enrolled in the last grade of primary education minus repeaters divided by the population in the relevant age cohort
5. Natural resource management	5. Eco-region protection, access to improved water, access to improved sanitation, and child (ages 1-4) mortality.
III. Encouraging Economic Freedom Category	
1. Inflation	1. The most recent 12-month change in consumer prices
2. Fiscal policy	2. Overall budget deficit divided by GDP, averaged over a 3-year period
3. Business start-up	3. Time and cost of complying with official procedures required for starting a business
4. Trade policy	4. Openness to international trade
5. Regulatory quality	5. Burden of regulation on business
6. Land rights and access	6. Secure land tenure, equitable access to land in rural areas, time and cost of property registration

Source: MCC (Guide).

country that passes the indicator test must develop a "compact" that details how it will spend MCA funds to increase its growth rate and reduce poverty, and that includes benchmarks to insure success. Recipient governments must design the compacts in consultation with their citizens, and they must implement, manage and maintain the development programs. MCC negotiation teams travel to each country to meet with members of the government and civil society in order to help design the compact. Each compact is reviewed by the MCC's board of directors. Once it is approved, the aid is delivered to the recipients.

In order to maintain eligibility for aid, recipient countries must continue to maintain and improve their overall performance on the indicators. MCC monitors the performance of recipient countries on the indicators throughout each year. A significant failure to maintain performance on the indicators can lead to a suspension of aid although a number of circumstances are identified that will not cause a suspension of aid if a country dips below the required indicator score. For example, a change in score due to the introduction of new indicators or new methodologies, or due to graduation from the low income category to the lower middle income category may cause a decrease in score that will not lead to a suspension of aid. On the other hand, in 2009, assistance for new activities in Nicaragua was suspended on the basis of concerns about the country's "commitment to democratic principles."

EVALUATION

The fundamental human problem treated in this book is using decentralization in order to satisfy the basic needs of the poor in a short time, so that they may contribute to the development process according to their potential, earn a decent living, and live a full life. The fundamental question of this section is: To what extent does MCA contribute to this objective? Let us use the World Bank's decentralization model of foreign aid to help answer this question.

Choose Recipient Countries Well

One objective of MCA is to make foreign aid more effective by choosing recipients that will use it well and by decentralizing planning and expenditure decisions to the recipient countries. In order to identify well-managed countries, MCC uses three categories of indicators (ruling justly, investing in people, and encouraging economic freedom) and requires recipients to achieve an above-the-median score on at least half the indicators of each category. Recipients must also control corruption and have a low per capita income. Does MCC succeed in identifying countries that deliver services effectively, not just in general, but specifically *to the poor*?

Ruling Justly?

To what extent do the indicators measure the justice of governance received, not by citizens in general, but *specifically by the poor*? To pass the governance test, a country must achieve an above-the-median score for the control of corruption and only two other governance indicators. The two additional indicators could be the rule of law and political rights. The law could be written by the wealthy and oriented toward preserving their short run economic interests. Similarly, the wealthy could control the political system through advertising, propaganda, lobbies, campaign contributions and other means, even though the poor may have the right to vote. This is especially possible in the extremely unequal countries of Latin America. Clearly, satisfying the governance indicators does not guarantee that *the poor* have a strong voice or client power or that government is effective in delivering basic goods and services to them.

Investing in People?

The satisfaction of basic needs is measured by the investment in people indicators. There are two indicators each for education and health, and one indicator for resource management. The resource management index is based on the factors, ecological protection, access to improved water and sanitation, and child mortality. Certainly, education and health are two services that are crucial for incorporating the poor into the development process, but a closer examination of the indicators shows that they do not guarantee that it is the poor who are being reached by the services.

Research by the World Bank has concluded that public spending on services in developing countries often fails to reach poor people (World Bank, 2003, pp. 38-40). In Ecuador, for example almost 40% of all health spending benefited the richest 20% of the population while less than 10% of the expenditures benefited the poorest 20% of the population (World Bank, 2003 Figure 2.5, p. 39). A country could gain approval for aid by above-the-median spending on education and health, and above-the-median immunization rates, none of which need benefit the poor very much.

Within the resource management category, access to improved water and sanitation, and child mortality are basic for enhancing the productivity of the poor. However, a country could avoid a very low score on natural resource management by ecological protection (that may actually make life more difficult for the poor) and gain approval for aid by supplying health and education services that benefit the poor very little.

The focus on health and education excludes from consideration many basic goods and services that may be essential for incorporating the poor into the development process such as roads, nutrition, housing and access to land. Limiting the sectors to education and health may also reduce the effectiveness of voice. The poor may communicate clearly to government a need for roads to transport their produce to market, but the government may have to respond: "Sorry. We have to supply education or health in order to get aid."

In general, the long list of factors that are used to construct the indicators include many basic goods and services that are crucial for enhancing the productivity of the poor. The trouble is that these factors can easily be avoided. It appears that a country can pass the aid test by doing quite little to satisfy the basic needs of the poor.

Encouraging Economic Freedom?

The indicators for economic freedom move beyond the service delivery model and aim to assure the freedom to invest and do business profitably in the recipient country. The first condition for doing business profitably is macroeconomic stability. The indicators that measure this include inflation and fiscal policy. Minimizing costly regulations and red tape are measured by regulatory quality and business start-up costs. A condition that may be especially beneficial to foreign investors is free international trade. It is noteworthy that free trade is not imposed upon the donors, but rather upon the developing countries receiving aid.

Looking back at the ruling justly indicators, we see that they too help to create an environment that is conducive to doing business profitably. The rule of law helps to assure the protection of private property, and the control of corruption lowers costs. A democratic political process guards against arbitrary and costly decisions of dictators.

The economic freedom indicators imply an approach to development. It is to work through the private sector to grow the economy and to let the resulting prosperity reduce poverty. Here, the private sector opens new businesses, hires people, and pays them a wage that can be used to satisfy basic needs. A more prosperous nation can afford to spend more on education, health and other basic goods and services.

Empirical studies support the private sector approach by finding a correlation between economic freedom and poverty reduction. The Heritage Foundation constructs an index of economic freedom based upon 50 variables. The 2001 edition of the Index of Economic Freedom concluded that "countries with the most economic freedom also have higher rates of long-term economic growth and are more prosperous than are those with less economic freedom" (O'Driscoll, Holmes, & Kirkpatrick, 2001, p. 1; cited in Pasicolan & Fitzgerald, 2002).

That this prosperity translates into the satisfaction of more basic needs is indicated by higher life expectancies for people living in more prosperous countries. Life expectancy, it will be remembered, is a proxy for having satisfied basic needs. Countries with a per capita income greater than $10,000 have an average life expectancy of 77.3 years; for countries with a per capita income less than $1,000, it is 56.0 years (World Bank, 2001c; cited in Pasicolan & Fitzgerald, 2002).

Balance?

The private sector approach to development is quite different from the approach implied by the service delivery model. The service delivery model focuses on making government effective in supplying basic goods and services to the poor so that they may realize their potential to contribute to the development process. The MCA approach is to rely on private investors to generate jobs. The model's approach is to prepare the poor to take them.

Both approaches have merit, and both are necessary. However, using only the private approach may take a very long time (centuries?) for general prosperity to filter down to the poorest of the poor. In principle, private markets will never supply public goods and services. Furthermore, as we saw in chapter 2, the impact of GNP growth on basic needs can be extremely variable depending, for example, on how employment-intensive the growth is, and whether the gains are channeled into remedying the deprivations of the neediest. Subsidizing business could siphon off funds that could be used more fruitfully by satisfying basic needs. There is a need to strike the balance between the two approaches that is most effective in satisfying the basic needs of the poor in a short time.

It may be argued that the greatest weakness of MCA is that it underemphasizes reliance on the public sector to deliver basic goods and services to the poor. The indicators amply protect private sector investors, but they do not assure that government effectively delivers the basic goods and services to the poor that are required to insure their full participation in the development process. One gets the impression that the designers of the program were more interested in fomenting U.S. business than in than in reducing poverty. Perhaps an imperfect ideology led to a well-intentioned overreliance on the private sector.

The policy implication is that the indicators for effective service delivery specifically *to the poor* should be strengthened. MCC could move in several directions to accomplish this. The first step would be to make satisfying the basic needs of the poor a priority that is at least as high as private sector development. Second, MCC could encourage the generation of more data on the poorest 25% of the population.

Third, MCC could revise the list of indicators for Investing in People. Access to improved water and sanitation and child mortality could be separated from protection of the ecology. A progressive tax indicator could be added for the reasons indicated in chapter 8 and to assure that the ruling classes of Latin America are doing their part. Land rights and access *of the poor* could be measured and moved from the encouraging economic freedom category to the investing in people category.

MCC continually strives to improve the indicators. It is not easy—outcomes can be difficult to measure, data can be missing or inaccurate, etc. An on-going challenge is to improve the investing in people indicators so that they guarantee the satisfaction of the basic needs of the poor that enhance their productivity and enable them to participate fully in the production process. It would be good to see MCC formally accept this challenge.

CONCLUSION

The extended service delivery model (as well as the empirical studies and World Bank experience upon which it is founded) teaches that the effectiveness of foreign aid can be improved by decentralizing planning and expenditures from donors to recipient nations that have effective service delivery systems. This contrasts sharply with the traditional approach of donors designing projects from afar and imposing multiple conditions upon recipients in order to assure that the projects are carried out. Incapacity and fungibility undermine the effectiveness of the traditional approach.

The most important contribution of the Millennium Challenge Account is to adopt the new approach to aid. MCA not only rewards effective management, it promotes their continual development. The median score on each indicator is (hopefully) an ever increasing number. In order to surpass it, countries must improve continually. MCA may establish a healthy competition between developing countries to improve their systems.

The main weakness of MCA is its failure to require recipient governments to develop an effective system for delivering basic goods and services specifically *to the poor*. There are ample requirements for establishing a context in which private enterprise can flourish, but there is a pressing need to improve the indicators so that they guarantee the satisfaction of the basic needs of the poor.

APPENDIX A: INDICATOR FACTORS[4]

Ruling Justly Category

- *Civil Liberties:* freedom of expression and belief, association and organizational rights, rule of law and human rights, personal autonomy, individual and economic rights, and the independence of the judiciary.
  Source: Freedom House
- *Political Rights:* prevalence of free and fair elections; the ability of citizens to form political parties that may compete fairly in elections; freedom from domination by the military, foreign powers, totalitarian parties, religious hierarchies and economic oligarchies; and the political rights of minority groups.
  Source: Freedom House
- *Voice and Accountability:* the extent to which a country's citizens are able to participate in selecting their government, as well as freedom of expression, freedom of association, and media independence.
  Source: World Bank Institute
- *Government Effectiveness*: the quality of public service provision, the quality of the civil service and its independence from political pressures, the quality of policy formulation and implementation, and the credibility of the government's commitment to such policies.
  Source: World Bank Institute
- *Rule of Law:* the extent to which individuals and firms have confidence in and abide by the rules of society; in particular, the quality of contract enforcement, the police, and the courts, as well as the likelihood of crime and violence.
  Source: World Bank Institute
- *Control of Corruption:* the extent to which public power is exercised for private grain, including both petty and grand forms of corruption, the "capture" of the state by elites and private interests, the effects of corruption on the business environment.
  Source: World Bank Institute

Investing in People Category

- *Public Expenditure on Health:* Total expenditures on health by government at all levels divided by gross domestic product.
  Source: The World Health Organization

- *Immunization Rates:* The average of DPT_3 and measles immunization rates for the most recent year available.
  Source: The World Health Organization
- *Total Public Expenditure on Primary Education:* Total expenditures on primary education by government at all levels divided by gross domestic product.
  Source: United Nations Educational Scientific and Cultural Organization
- *Girls' Primary Completion Rate:* The number of female students enrolled in the last grade of primary education minus repeaters divided by the population in the relevant age cohort.
  Source: United Nations Educational Scientific and Cultural Organization
- *Natural Resource Management:* Eco-region protection, access to improved water, access to improved sanitation, and child (ages 1-4) mortality.
  Sources: The Center for International Earth Science Information Network and the Yale Center for Environmental Law and Policy

Encouraging Economic Freedom Category

- *Inflation:* The most recent 12-month change in consumer prices.
  Source: The International Monetary Fund's World Economic Outlook database
- *Fiscal Policy:* The overall budget deficit divided by gross domestic product, averaged over a 3-year period.
  Sources: International Monetary Fund Country Reports, National Governments, and the International Monetary Fund's World Economic Outlook database
- *Business Start-Up:* The time and cost of complying with all procedures officially required for an entrepreneur to start up and formally operate an industrial or commercial business.
  Source: International Finance Corporation
- *Trade Policy:* Weighted average tariff rates and nontariff barriers to trade.
  Source: The Heritage Foundation
- *Regulatory Quality:* The burden of regulations on business, price controls, the government's role in the economy, foreign investment regulation, and many other areas.
  Source: World Bank Institute

- *Land Rights and Access:* the extent to which the institutional, legal, and market framework provide secure land tenure and equitable access to land in rural areas and the time and cost of property registration in urban and per-urban areas.
  Sources: The International Fund for Agricultural Development and the International Finance Corporation

NOTES

1. The definitions of foreign aid are derived from World Bank 2003, Box 3, p. 6.
2. The model is based on World Bank, 2003, Chapter 11.
3. Unless otherwise indicated, the description of the Millennium Challenge Account is drawn from its web site, <http://www.mcc.gov>.
4. The sources for the Appendix are: MCC, Guide, pp. 7-35; MCC (2008), pp. 6-8.

CONCLUSION

Poverty and inequality are widespread throughout Latin America. More than one in five Latin Americans live on less than $2 a day. Countless more are condemned to living on $3, $5, or $10 a day. Latin America is also the most unequal region in the world. Given its low per capita income (approximately one sixth that of the United States), extreme inequality implies dire poverty for those at the bottom of the income scale.

The best solution to the poverty and inequality of Latin America includes satisfying the needs of the poor for basic education, health, nutrition, and other goods and services. Satisfying basic needs renders the poor more productive, and it creates new opportunities to earn the income necessary to escape poverty and live a full life.

But satisfying basic needs does more than empower the poor to escape poverty. It develops the *nation*. Making the poor more productive speeds the growth of gross domestic product, so that more goods and services are available for consumption. It lowers the costs of production thus increasing profits and lowering prices. Satisfying basic needs tends to lower taxes by reducing the need for public welfare expenditures and for public expenditures to combat crime.

Decentralization—the progressive process of transferring taxing and spending decisions from the central government to subnational governments—can help to satisfy basic needs in many important ways. First, it can strengthen the nation's system of delivering basic goods and services.

Decentralization for Satisfying Basic Needs: An Economic Guide for Policymakers, 2nd Edition
pp. 165–170

Bringing government closer to the poor can overcome one of the most destructive aspects of poverty, voicelessness. Strengthening the voice of the poor can improve the compact between policymakers and providers through providing input of the poor into the planning process. Hearing the voice of the people can enable subnational governments to tailor expenditures to meet the varying needs of the poor across jurisdictions, and it can help to secure optimum quantities of public goods and services.

Decentralization can increase client power and so marshal more participation of the poor in the production of basic goods and services, improve monitoring and reduce corruption. Voice and client power together enable the poor to become more active subjects who determine their own destinies, something that is of itself one of the most fundamental basic needs. Decentralizing taxing and spending can develop the expertise of subnational agents who "learn on the job."

However, for decentralization to have positive effects on the satisfaction of basic needs, the circumstances in which it takes place must be propitious. These circumstances include an approximately optimum distribution of income, a healthy political system, and sound administrative capacity on every level of government.

If the circumstances are ideal, the way to decentralize is to simply "devolve" taxing and spending to the level of government that approximately "corresponds" to the areas encompassing the beneficiaries. Since the distribution of income is optimum, the type and quantity of each public good and service is then determined by citizen demand. The role of each level of government is to respond by supplying the public goods and services demanded, and by taxing the citizens in order to pay for it. This yields the welfare maximizing quantities of all public goods and services for each jurisdiction, including those supplied to the (relatively) poor.

The problem is that real world circumstances are less than ideal. Instead of an optimum distribution of income, inequality is extreme throughout Latin America. The political system is often controlled by elites and beset by corruption. Administrative capacity, especially of states and municipalities, is often weak.

In the real world, devolution can actually undermine the satisfaction of basic needs and slow the creation of an inclusive development process. For example, devolving taxing and spending from a pro-poor central government to local governments controlled by elites could result in a more regressive tax system and fewer basic goods and services supplied to the poor.

The challenge is to design a constructive decentralization process in the context of imperfect circumstances. It is necessary to work one's way through imperfect, real world circumstances towards the ideal of devolution. This makes the process of decentralization much more challenging than it would be in a simple, ideal world. What can be done in the "here and now" to advance the process of decentralization toward the ideal?

There is no simple formula that can be applied mindlessly. Analysis and entrepreneurship are essential. The first step is to analyze the strengths and weaknesses of the service delivery system at each level of government, viz., of the agents (citizens/poor, politicians/policymakers, and providers), and their relationships (voice, compact, and client power). Are the assumptions of the model satisfied?

The second step is to design a degree of political, fiscal and administrative decentralization that exploits the strengths, that helps to overcome the weaknesses, and that compensates for its temporarily insurmountable or low-priority weaknesses. Chapter 4 can help in this endeavor. Table 4.1 summarizes the degrees of decentralization. Table 4.2 identifies the principal strengths and weaknesses of each degree and type.

The third step is to implement the planned advance in decentralization. This requires entrepreneurship that can be practiced by all agents of the service delivery system including the poor.

The cases of chapters 5-10 illustrate this process at work. The first case was Mexico's transfer-led decentralization. Mexico centralized taxes in response to the fiscal chaos that existed at the state and local levels of government. It "delegated" spending and administration in order to exploit the relative capacity of states and municipalities to take into account the specific needs of their jurisdictions and to carry out projects.

Delegating the administration of the FAIS grant for social infrastructure to municipalities with notoriously weak administrative capacities seems to manifest a faith in their abilities to learn by doing. An objective of helping the poor become subjects of their own futures seems to be manifested in the guidelines that require the promotion of the full participation of the poor in every phase of supplying the infrastructure.

The main strengths of Mexico's transfer-led decentralization is the capacity for redistribution that comes from centralized and progressive taxation. Its main weaknesses include a failure to take sufficient advantage of that capacity for redistribution, weak voice, and a failure create a broad, comprehensive plan for satisfying basic needs within a short period of time.

Mexico could deepen its current stage of decentralization by raising more funds for the satisfaction of basic needs through progressive taxation. It should construct a comprehensive plan to satisfy basic needs within a short period of time and begin to implement it by coordinating the many agencies that supply basic goods and services to the poor.

Mexico could advance to a higher degree of decentralization through improving the administrative capacity of municipalities and by delegating more spending responsibilities to them, especially in the areas of primary education and basic health services.

Chapter 6 considered the case of Mexico's *Oportunidades* program that delivers a package of education, health and nutrition benefits to "extremely poor" households of rural areas. Planning and finance are centralized, and delivery is carried out by deconcentrated offices of the central government.

The program shows that central government can have a significant planning advantage over state and local governments: it can employ top experts to develop a sophisticated plan for satisfying basic needs, and it can raise the revenues necessary to implement the plan. Deconcentrated offices can draw on existing agencies with experience and expertise in delivering the services.

The price of price of this highly centralized approach is weak voice and client power. The poor are left as quite passive consumers of the benefits bestowed by the federal government. Weak voice tends to exclude variations in benefits according to need across jurisdictions. Weak client power tends to weaken monitoring and the participation of the poor in the development process. Another weakness of the program is that it creates additional demand for services without adding to their supply.

It could be argued that *Oportunidades* is preparing the poor to take charge of their lives. After they are educated, healthy and nourished, they can be more forthright in expressing their voice, their client power, and so on. Hopefully, this is true, but decentralizing some aspects of the program now may strengthen its impact. For example, involving the poor in monitoring could improve delivery. Inviting the participation of the poor in producing the goods and services could increase supply at a low cost.

Chapter 7 presented the very interesting case of the state of Tlaxcala, Mexico, that decentralized by creating a fourth level of government, community governments. The community governments are legally subordinate to their municipalities, but they elect their own authorities, identify and prioritize their own needs for public services, plan their own development projects, and receive federal grants to carry out their projects.

The fascinating advantage of Tlaxcala's approach to decentralization is that it very much enhances the voice and client power of the "voiceless" poor. Ready or not, low-income citizens are by necessity transformed into very active participants in the development of their communities. The literature reports surprising results of decentralizing to the level of the municipality. It will be interesting to watch the impact on basic goods and services generated by the communities.

The main challenge that the community governments may face is that they place very heavy reliance on volunteers, and that the volunteers may have limited administrative capacity. Also, it is not clear that Tlaxcala took into account the principle of correspondence or the costs of supplying basic goods and services when it formed its community governments.

The next step for Tlaxcala may be to develop administrative capacity on the community level and to coordinate development projects between communities. There may also be a need to redefine the jurisdictions of some communities. Certainly, the principle of correspondence should be considered in forming new community governments.

Taxation is important for satisfying basic needs because it provides the funds necessary for both the government and the poor to purchase the basic goods and services that enhance productivity and generate an inclusive development process. Chapter 8 argued that in the context of Latin America's extreme poverty and inequality, the best fiscal system is to centralize progressive taxes and decentralize the supply of basic goods and services to the poor. This makes it possible to carry out the necessary redistribution of income and to achieve relative efficiency in supplying basic goods and services.

The World Bank has despaired of imposing progressive taxes in Latin America and, in order to increase government revenues and spending, it has recommended enforcing more regressive tax systems. It is unlikely that this reduces tax evasion by the ruling class. Any additional revenues are likely to come from the middle class and the poor. If so, the result will be a deepening and prolongation of extreme inequality. If the ruling class cannot be taxed to satisfy the basic needs of the poor, it is unlikely that, after having strengthened its control of society, it can be convinced to dedicate itself to spending government funds to satisfy those needs.

The World Bank should change its primary tax objective from "raising revenues" to "raising revenues for the basic needs of the poor through progressive taxation." It can begin to implement this policy by assisting an attack on tax evasion by the ruling class, by recommending increases in the maximum marginal rates of the income taxes, and decreases in dependence on the regressive value added tax. In addition, recommending greater reliance on the inheritance, gift and other wealth taxes is crucial. The World Bank should be supported in this endeavor by contributing governments and by political movements at home.

Chapter 9 explored the effects on El Salvador of having followed the World Bank tax advice. The tax system of El Salvador has remained highly regressive after implementing the World Bank tax advice, although the percentage of total tax revenues raised by regressive indirect taxes has fallen somewhat. Since the ruling class appears to be evading its taxes, the tax system has probably been made more regressive in the all-important upper income range. Regressivity in the upper income range has been significantly worsened by eliminating the crucial inheritance and gift taxes, and possibly by eliminating the national property tax. The rate of growth of revenues and expenditures on health and education rose in the early years of the reform and then fell. Hence, the long-run effect of the World Bank tax advice may be to slow the growth of revenues and expenditures, and to deepen and prolong an extreme inequality that obstructs the satisfaction of the basic needs necessary for generating an inclusive development process.

The policy recommendation for El Salvador is similar to that made in Chapter 8 for all developing countries. El Salvador should change its primary tax objective from "raising revenues" to "raising revenues for the basic needs of the poor through progressive taxation." It should attack tax evasion by the ruling class, increase the maximum marginal rates of the income taxes, and decrease dependence on the regressive value added tax. It is crucial to restore and increase the inheritance and gift taxes, and the national property tax. The politicians of El Salvador are trying to function in a country with a long history of violent oppression in order to maintain the dominance of the ruling class. They require the support of the international community and local political movements in order to create a tax system that fosters the satisfaction of basic needs and inclusive development.

Chapter 10 showed that the United States is decentralizing its foreign aid by directing it towards countries that are able and willing to use it "well" and by devolving planning and spending to the recipients. Performance indicators are used to determine whether the countries are worthy of aid.

The main advantage of this approach is that it frees recipient countries to draw on their superior knowledge of their circumstances to design and implement their own programs for satisfying basic needs. It is difficult to manage the world from Washington.

The main disadvantage of the program is that the performance indicators are heavily biased toward creating a favorable business climate. They are inadequate for determining country success in satisfying the basic needs of the poor.

Future steps for this program should include improving the indicators to reveal achievements in satisfying basic goods and services specifically of the poor. Creating a favorable business climate is good up to a point, but we also need to know whether the country is preparing the poor to participate in the business world.

Inclusive development through satisfying the basic needs of Latin America's poor is an urgent challenge. Decentralization can be a significant help in meeting this challenge. If this book improves the reader's understanding of how the process of decentralization can work to satisfy the basic needs of the poor, and if it enhances his or her skills at putting it to work, it will have accomplished its objective.

REFERENCES

Aghón, G. (1993). *Descentralización Fiscal: Marco Conceptual.* Santiago: Naciones Unidas Comisión Económica para América Latina y El Caribe.

Banco Central de Reserva de El Salvador. Índice de Precios al Consumidor, Global y por Divisiones, Variación Anual, desde 1994. Retrieved from http://www.bcr.gob.sv/Estadísticas/Series Estadísticas/

Bureau of Economic Analysis. (2009). *Current and real dollar GDP.* Retrieved from http://www.bea.doc.gov

Behrman, J., & Hoddinott, J. (2000, July) An evaluation of the impact of PROGRESA on preschool child height. *FCND Research Theme.* International Food Policy Research Institute. Retrieved from http://www.ifpri.org/themes/progresa.htm

Blandón de Grajeda, F. (2003, October). *Algunos apuntes sobre desarrollo local y descentralización.* El Salvador: Universidad Centroamericana José Simeón Cañas: Estudios Centroamericanos.

Centro de Información, Documentación y Apoyo a la Investigación de la Universidad Centroamericana José Simeón Cañas. (2008). Corrupción y Evasión fiscal en El Salvador. *Proceso, 28,* 1275-1281.

CEPALSTAT. (2009). Retrieved from http://www.eclac.org/estadisticas/default.asp?idioma=IN

Chhibber, A., & Khalilzadeh-Shirazi, J. (1988). *Public finances in adjustment programs. Pre-working Paper 128.* Washington, DC: World Bank, Country Economics Department.

Coady, D. P. (2001, May). *An evaluation of the distributional power of PROGRESA's cash transfers in Mexico.* Retrieved from http://www.ifpri.org/themes/progresa.htm

Collier, P., & Dollar, D. (1998). *Aid allocation and poverty reduction.* Washington, DC: World Bank, Development Research Group.

Congressional Budget Office. (2009). *Revenues, outlays, surpluses, deficits, and debt held by the public: Percentage of gross domestic product.* Retrieved from http://www.cbo.gov

Constitución Política del Estado Libre y Soberano del Estado de Tlaxcala. (1998, September). Retrieved from http://www.tsjtlaxcala.gob.mx

Drèze, J., & Sen, A. (1995). *India: Economic development and social Opportunity.* Oxford, England: Clarendon Press.

Franco, P. (2003). *The puzzle of Latin American economic development* (2nd ed.) New York, NY: Rowman & Littlefield..

Gershberg, A., & Winkler, D. (2000). Education decentralization in Latin America: The effects on the quality of schooling. In B. S. Javed, F. Eid, M. E. Freire, V. Vergra, & G.E. Perry (Eds.), *Proceedings of the annual World Bank Conference on Development in Latin America and the Caribbean 1999.* Washington, DC: World Bank.

Giugale, M. M., & Webb, S. B. (Eds.). (2000, May). Achievements and challenges of fiscal decentralization: Lessons from Mexico. *The World Bank.* Retrieved from http://www.worldbank.org

Hicks, N. (1979). Growth vs. basic needs: Is there a trade-off? *World Development, 7,* 985-994.

Hoddinott, J., Skoufias, E. & Washburn, R. (2000, September) The impact of PROGRESA on consumption: A final report. *International Food Policy Research Institute.* Retrieved from http://www.ifpri.org/themes/progresa.htm

Inter-American Development Bank. (1996). *Economic and social progress in Latin America: 1996 report.* Baltimore, MD: The Johns Hopkins University Press.

International Monetary Fund. (various years). *Government finance statistics yearbook.* Washington, DC: Author.

Knight, J. B., Sabot, R. H., & Hovey, D. C. (1992, August). Is the rate of return on primary schooling really 26 per cent? *Journal of African Economies, 1,* 2, 192-205.

Ley de Coordinación Fiscal. (2009, June). *Cámara de Diputados del H. Congreso de la Unión.* Retrieved from http://www.diputados.gob.mx/LeyesBiblio/pdf/31.pdf

Ley Orgánica Municipal del Estado de Tlaxcala. *SEGOB* (Secretaría de Gobernación de México). Retrieved from http://www.tsjtlaxcala.gob.mx

Lindert, P., & Pugel, T.L. (1996). *International economics* (10th ed.). Chicago, IL: Irwin.

McConnell, C. R., Brue, S. L., & Flynn S. M. (2009). *Economics: Principles, problems and policies* (18th ed.). New York, NY: McGraw-Hill Irwin.

McGuire, J. M. (1990, Noviembre-Diciembre). Los cambios de la estructura tributaria de El Salvador: implicaciones para el desarrollo. *Realidad Económico-Social, 3*(18), 641-676.

Mexican Economic Report. (2004, June). *Lloyd.* Retrieved from http://www.lloyd.com.mx/en/reportes/June.pdf

Millennium Challenge Corporation. (2008, October). *Report on the criteria and methodology for determining the eligibility of candidate countries for Millennium Challenge Account assistance in fiscal year 2009.* Retrieved from http://www.mcc.gov/selection/indicators/index.php

Millennium Challenge Corporation (n.d.-a). *Guide to the MCC indicators and the selection process: Fiscal year 2009.* Retrieved from http://www. mca.go v/documents/mcc-fy08-guidetoindicatorsandtheselectionprocess.pdf

Millennium Challenge Corporation. (n.d.-b). MCC in Latin America. Retrieved from http://www.mcc.gov/mcc/panda/activities/latinamerica/ index.shtml

Ministerio de Hacienda de El Salvador. (1987). *Manual de Clasificación de Ingresos.* San Salvador, El Salvador: Dirección de Planificación Fiscal.

Ministerio de Hacienda de El Salvador. (n.d.). *Glosario.* Retrieved from http:// www.mh. gov.sv

Ministerio de Hacienda de El Salvador. (n.d.) *Impuestos internos.* Retrieved from http://www.mh.gob.sv/portal/page?_pageid=182,1&_dad=portal &_schema=PORTAL

Morley, S. A. (1995). *Poverty and inequality in Latin America: The impact of adjustment and recovery in the 1980s.* Baltimore, MD: The Johns Hopkins University Press.

Musgrave, R. A., & Musgrave, P. B. (1989). *Public finance in theory and practice* (5th ed.). St. Louis, MO: McGraw-Hill.

Nafziger, E. W. (1997). *The economics of developing countries* (3rd ed.). Englewood Cliffs, NJ: Prentice Hall.

Narayan, D., Patel, R., Schafft, K., Rademacher, A., & Koch-Schulte, S. (2000). *Voices of the poor: Can anyone hear us?* New York, NY: Oxford University Press.

Newbery, D., & Stern, N. (Eds.). (1987). *The theory of taxation for developing countries.* New York, NY: Oxford University Press.

Oates, W. E. (1972). *Fiscal federalism.* New York: Harcourt Brace Jovanovich.

O'Driscoll, G. P., Jr., Holmes, K. R., & Kirkpatrick, M. (2001). *Index of economic freedom.* Washington, DC: Heritage Foundation and Dow Jones & Company.

Organization for Economic Cooperation and Development. (2008). *Factbook 2008: Economic, environmental and social statistics.* Retrieved from http://www.oecd.org/ dataoecd/48/4/37867909.pdf

Organization for Economic Cooperation and Development. (2009a). *Net official development assistance for 2008.* Retrieved from http://www.oecd.org/dataoecd/ 48/34/42459170.pdf>.

Organization for Economic Cooperation and Development. (2009b.) *Gross bilateral ODA, 2006-2007 Average.* Retrieved from http://www.oecd.org/dataoecd/42/30 /41732048.jpg

Olmedo Carranza, R. (1999). *El Poder Comunitario en Tlaxcala: Las Presidencias Municipales Auxiliares.* México DF: Editorial Comuna.

Pasicolan, P., & Fitzgerald, S. (2002, October 18). The Millennium Challenge Account: Linking aid with economic freedom. *The Heritage Foundation, Policy Research and Analysis.* Retrieved from http://www.heritage.org/Research /TradeandForeignAid/bg1602.cfm

Plan Estatal de Desarrollo 1999-2005. (1998). *Estado de Tlaxcala, Coordinación General de Informática.* Retrieved from http://www.tlaxcala.gob.mx/portal/plan/ plandesarrollo.html

Psacharopoulos, G. (1994). Returns to investment in education: A global update. *World Development, 22,* 1325-1343.

Raich, U. (2005). *Impactos de la descentralización del gasto en los municipios mexicanos.* Retrieved from http://www.transparencia.org.mx/docs/descentralizacion.pdf

Random House. (1991). *Webster's college dictionary*. New York, NY: McGraw-Hill.

Rey de Marulanda, N. (1996). Taxation in Latin America and the Caribbean: Achievements and outlook. Chapter 1 in Inter-American Development Bank (1996) *Reform of tax administration in Latin America: Progress and perspectives*. Washington, DC: Inter-American Development Bank.

Rieffel, L., & Fox, J. W. (2008, December). The Millennium Challenge Corporation: An opportunity for the next president. *Global Economy and Development*. Working Paper 30. Retrieved from http://www.brookings.edu/papers/2008/12_mcc_rieffel.aspx

Rosen, H. S. (2005). *Public finance* (7th ed.). St. Louis, MO: McGraw-Hill Irwin.

Sachs, J. D., & Larrain, B. F. (1993). *Macroeconomics in the global economy*. Englewood Cliffs, NJ: Prentice Hall.

Scott, J. (2001, May 14). *High inequality, low revenue: Redistributive efficiency of Latin American fiscal policy in comparative perspective*. Retrieved from http://www.iadb.org

Secretaría de Desarrollo Social. (2009a). *Monto de los Apoyos*. Retrieved from http://www.oportunidades.gob.mx

Secretaría de Desarrollo Social. (2009b). *¿Quiénes Somos?* Retrieved from http://www.oportunidades.gob.mx

Secretaría de Desarrollo Social. (2009c). Retrieved from http://www.oportunidades.gob.mx/Wn_Jovenes/index.html

Secretaría de Desarrollo Social. (2009d). *Cuadernillo de Información del Programa Oportunidades para Directores y Docentes de Educación Básica*. Retrieved from http://www.oportunidades.gob.mx

Secretaría de Desarrollo Social. (2009e). *Controlaría Social a través de los Comités de Promoción Communitaria*. Retrieved from http://www. oportunidades.gob.mx

Shah, A. (2008, April 27). Foreign aid numbers in charts and graphs. *Global Issues*. Retrieved from http://www.globalissues.org/Foreign Aid

Skoufias, E. (2000, May). The education, health and nutrition (PROGRESA) program of Mexico. *International Food Policy Research Institute*. Retrieved from http://www.ifpri.org/themes/progresa.htm

Skoufias, E. (2001, December). *PROGRESA and its impacts on the human capital and welfare of households in rural Mexico: A synthesis of the results of an evaluation by IFPRI*. Retrieved from http://www.ifpri.org/themes/progresa.htm

Skoufias, E., Davis, B., & Behrman, J.R. (1999, June). *Final report: An Evaluation of the selection of beneficiary households in the education, health, and nutrition program (PROGRESA) of Mexico*. Retrieved from http://www.ifpri.org/themes/progresa.htm

Stewart, F. (1985). *Basic needs in developing countries*. Baltimore, MD: The Johns Hopkins University Press.

Stiglitz, J., & Bilmes, L. (2008, March 9). The Iraq war will cost us $3 trillion, and much more. *The Washington Post Online*. Retrieved from http://www.washingtonpost.com/wp-dyn/content/article/2008/03/07/AR2008030702846.html

Streeten, P., Burki, S. J., Haq, M. U., Hicks, N., & Stewart, F. (1981). *First things first: Meeting basic human needs in developing countries*. New York, NY: Oxford University Press.

Székely, M., & Hilgert, M. (1999, December). *What is behind the inequality we measure: An investigation using Latin American data?* Inter-American Development Bank Research Department Working Paper #409. Retrieved from http://idbdocs.iadb.org/wsdpcs/getdocumentaspx?docnum=788227

Tait, A. A. (1967). *The taxation of personal wealth*. Chicago: University of Illinois Press.

Tanzi, V. (1996). Tax reform in Latin America in the past decade in Inter-American Development Bank. *Reform of Tax Administration in Latin America*, pp. 17-37.

Thirsk, W. (Ed.). (1997). *Tax reform in developing countries.* Washington, DC: The World Bank.

Trigueros, A. A. *Respondiendo a los desafíos fiscales en El Salvador.* San Salvador, El Salvador: FUSADES, Estudios estratégicos, Departamento de Estudios Económicos y Sociales.

United Nations. (2000). *Human development report 2000: Human rights and human development.* New York, NY: Oxford University Press.

United Nations. (2003). *Human development report 2003: Millennium development goals: A compact among nations to end human poverty.* New York, NY: Oxford University Press.

United Nations. (2004). *Human development report 2004: Cultural liberty in today's diverse world*. New York, NY: Oxford University Press.

United Nations. (2007/2008). *Human development report 2007/2008: Fighting climate change: Human solidarity in a divided world*. New York, NY: Oxford University Press.

World Bank. (1990). *World debt tables 1990-91* (Vol. 2., country tables). Washington, DC: Author.

World Bank. (1991). *Lessons of tax reform.* Washington, DC: Author.

World Bank. (1992). *World development report 1992: Development and the environment.* Washington, DC: Author.

World Bank. (1996). *World debt tables 1996* (Vol. 2., country tables). Washington, DC: Author.

World Bank. (1998). Assessing aid: What works, what doesn't, and why. *Aid Effectiveness Research.*Washington, DC: Author. Retrieved from http://www.worldbank.org

World Bank. (2001). *World development indicators 2001*. Washington, DC: Author.

World Bank. (2003). *World development report 2004: Making services work for poor people.* Washington, DC: The World Bank.

World Bank. (2009). *Designing Tax structure.* Retrieved from http://www.worldbank.org

World Wide Military Expenditures. (2009). Retrieved from http://www.globalsecurity.org/military/world/spending.htm

ABOUT THE AUTHOR

James Michael McGuire is a professor of economics at the University of the Incarnate Word, San Antonio, Texas where he teaches public finance, international economics, and Latin American economics. He was a Fulbright Scholar to the Central American University José Simeón Cañas (UCA) of El Salvador, 1989-1991. He returns to El Salvador each summer to conduct research and to teach economics in the UCA's Master of Business Administration Program. His research focuses on the public finance of inclusive development of Latin America.

INDEX

www.ingramcontent.com/pod-product-compliance
Lightning Source LLC
LaVergne TN
LVHW011130300926
849160LV00008B/593